Business School for Busy Business Owners

Year One

And you thought You Were too busy Running Your Business to Go to Business School

50 Must read, short to the point and entertaining mini business school lessons that will help catapult your small business to the next level

Tim Hmelar

Palo Alto, CA

ISBN: 978-0-578-10967-7

Printed in the United States

Warning: Any and all legal, accounting or financial advice provided herein is general in nature and not intended to apply to your particular situation. You should seek the advice of an attorney or accountant licensed to practice law in the state or country where you reside.

"Its not a matter of getting out of your "comfort zone" – most people are not living a comfortable or fulfilling life; it's a matter of MAKING THE DECISION to get out of your "familiar zone", by overcoming your fears and lack of enthusiasm for life and then writing and implementing your own life plan."

-Tim Hmelar

Dedication & Acknowledgements:

Dedication:

This book is dedicated to every biz person, whether successful or not, who has had the courage to try to start and run a business. Without all you dreamers, job creators, inventors, optimists and believers, this country would not be what it is today. May your spirit glow brightly, may you have the wisdom to dream and pursue your business goals with confidence, intelligence and logic, may you find the time to always share your talents with others, and may you find the wind of negative naysayers always at your back.

A special shout out to Monica, Fe, Seattle and Gracia, my Grandmother Gertrude, my Mom and Dad, and to my brothers and sisters, Steve, Frank, Anni, Lisa, Michael and Sue. In memory of Angel Ortiz, a friend, a true entrepreneur, one of the kindest people I ever met, a giver and a seeker of truth – you will be missed – vaya con Dios.

Acknowledgements:

Special thanks to everyone along my entrepreneurial path, with special thanks to Bob Noyce, Pitch Johnson, Jack Falvey, David Ungerer, Wanda Blockhus, Nancy Chillag, Guy Kawasaki, Nick Ross, Gary Vaynerchuk, Paul Allen, Jon Jantsch, Bill Rancic, Bernie Marcus, Rob Mori, Bob Parsons, Daffy Dave, Clark Kepler, Gino Blefari, Karen Salmansohn, JP Garcia, Harry Corbett, John Thompson, Tom Tognoli, Mia Kim Park, Pam Rodgers, Michael Stelzner, Ken Yap, Jurgen Weller, Ronald Mueller, Bradon

Marshall, Andrea Maldonado, Jenn Rhodes, Oscar Garcia, Nina Sidhu, Thomas Sullivan, Michael Spain, Diana Estrada, Dave Kupec, Lia Strelow, Kent Vickery, Don Long, Anni Hmelar, Stephen Hmelar Jr., Debra Cen, Jonathan Pitts, Neil Schwartz, Eric Haas, Marie Forleo, Shashank Shekhar, Andrew Litt and Abuelita Maria.

Why You Should Read This Book and Why Tim Hmelar is qualified to Write It

The vast majority of small business owners and managers I know are business owners by default. They own or manage a business they never expected to have and somehow they woke one morning and wala (yes, I know its French and is actually spelled voila); they found themself at the wheel of a small business bus trying to manage a business with no instruction manual. If you find yourself in one of the following situations this book is for you:

In a moment of insanity did you decide to start a business?
Did you turn your hobby or passion into a business?
Are you a stay at home Mom or Dad who needs more cash to take care of your family?
Did you get laid off and nobody will hire you?
Are you a member of the lucky sperm club and you inherited the family business?
Did you start a business with one of your friends?
Would you like to generate more income so you can retire?
Do you manage a business for someone else?
Are you a great cook or construction worker or other blue collar worker and somehow you went from cooking and building to running a business?
Want more time to spend with your family and less with your business?
Thinking of starting a business so that you can maintain your lifestyle as you age?

If you answered yes to any of the above questions; this book is for you.

Let me introduce myself. My name is Tim Hmelar (last name pronounced Mil-lar), I'm 54 and I live in Palo Alto, CA. I'm a family man, have 3 children, and a serial entrepreneur who has never worked for anyone else except myself since the age of 19.

I studied Small Business and Entrepreneurship at San Jose State University and financed my education by painting and remodeling homes. During my junior year in college I took a semester off from school to help my brother Frank orchestrate a leveraged buy-out of a plastics company in Sudbury, Massachusetts. I literally combed through my text books in Finance, Law, Accounting, Statistics and Operations Research to help my brother with his successful purchase, re-location and laying out of his business.

After graduating from school (FYI, it took me 8 years to get my bachelor's degree) I got my General Contractors license and started remodeling homes in Palo Alto, CA. While managing my company I also worked my butt off to systemize and make my company as efficient as possible. I worked on some of the wealthiest people's homes in the world and even managed a job in Costa Rica. I studied software development, became fluent in Spanish and soaked up everything I could about small business management and social media. I started a business called Web Lunch Box and worked with over 300 businesses helping them set up their social media campaigns. I even helped one friend, Daffy Dave, with his social media strategy who now gets over 1,000,000 hits/month from his YouTube Channel.

Besides my business success I've had some business failures, I tried for two years to set up a real estate business in Mexico just as the U.S. mortgage system crashed and nearly bankrupted the U.S. economy. I also started an online coupon company as I watched Groupon signs go up down the street from where I live.

So why listen to me, I've had business successes and failures that you hopefully can learn from. I've learned from my experiences, both good and bad, and believe this book can save you money, time, maybe help make you rich, may save your marriage and hopefully help make your business dreams come true.

Why Did I Write - Business School for Busy Business People: Year One?

I decided to write this book after spending two years of my life working with hundreds of struggling small business owners. Most of these business owners felt extremely negative about the future of their businesses, felt that the mortgage industry and Wall Street had driven the U.S. economy into a financial ditch, and felt that the wars in Iraq and Afghanistan would never be won.

Americans were worried about how they would retire, how they would get medical care as they aged, and they wondered if Obama could salvage America's future like Harry Houdini performing a magic trick. They were worried about how they would pay for their kid's college educations and even more worried if there would be jobs for their kids after attending college. They also were pissed off at every single politician in Washington, DC. They believed that if they personally had to operate within a family budget and live without a retirement account, how come Washington was oblivious to the pain they were feeling and how come our elected officials and government workers received killer salaries, pensions and benefits. Independent small business owners on Main Street, USA were down and out, depressed and pissed off.

I served on the board of Home Town Peninsula, a Menlo Park, CA organization that promotes buying from local businesses. I taught seminars about social media and conducted classes to home owners on how to remodel their homes. I had the scare of my life when I had to have a tumor removed from back; and I watched a friend, Clark Kepler, get out of the 50 year old family-run book selling business when he realized many of the people frequenting his store were just there to browse through a book before buying it on Amazon.com.

On one hand, I saw my construction friends lose their businesses and homes; and on the other, I witnessed a wave of foreign investors buy the majority of real estate for sale in the town where I live. I wondered how so much economic activity could be happening where there were such big winners and so many big losers.

I re-accessed everything I was doing in business. Was I focusing my time and effort on the right things? How would I use my business to pay for my kid's college education? How was I going to retire and where? I even had a come-to-Jesus meeting with my family about my business decisions. It was at this time I realized I needed to focus on business fundamentals I had learned so long ago at San Jose State University. I needed to focus on cash flow, minimizing expenses, marketing and creating great customer experiences and had to start saying NO to anything that was sucking my time away from my family and my business. I had to cut back on my involvement on managing school events; I told my friends *"No I don't have the time to meet and hear about your new business activities."* And I had to sit down and write a new plan for my family's future. It was humbling to say the least.

I came to the conclusion that the majority of small businesses on every single Main Street in America must be struggling to survive. The one advantage I had over many of my fellow brother and sister small business owners was that I had 30 years of small business management experience and a degree in

Business Administration with a concentration in Small Business and Entrepreneurship. It was at this time I had an epiphany. My friends needed a business degree and didn't have the time or money to go. They were overwhelmed running their businesses, their health and bank accounts were suffering, many were approaching an age where nobody would hire them at a position that paid more than minimum wage and they were scared silly. They needed to go to business school, they had no time and their business needed a lobotomy.

It was at this time I came up with the idea to write **_Business School for Busy Business Owners_**. Instead of holding class in large lecture halls each of my students could attend class while sitting at their kitchen table or on their porcelain throne. I also learned I have enough content to write a follow up book for the second year of business school. I decided to call my book **Business School for Busy Business Owners - Year One**. I hope you find this book informative and entertaining and most of all helpful in managing your business. I'd love to hear your stories and comments. Let class begin!

To Your Success,

Tim Hmelar

Palo Alto, CA   May 2014

Contents

Marketing & Sales

Do You Have the Gift of Gab? Or Do You Have Big Balls? Marketing vs. Sales

Assuming that you have the necessary skill to offer a service or have the capability of building and distributing a product, there is no skill more important to the survival of your business than marketing. Marketing is the orchestrated effort that tells people about your business product or service. If people don't know your business exists, don't know about your product, and if they don't trust you, you will be spinning your wheels and going broke. All businesses need to continuously market themselves. Most marketing people tend to be creative and have the GIFT OF GAB. They love to tell people how wonderful their product or service is.

Some old school examples of marketing are as simple as having a business card, a sign on your car/truck, ads in the paper, fliers distributed to targeted customers, attending network groups such as BNI, or having a booth at a trade show. In the last 10 years, the world of marketing was turned on its head with the arrival of social media. New school marketing tools include having profiles on Facebook, Twitter, Google, Merchant Circle, Pinterest, and other social networking sites where lots of people spend their time online every day. It also includes exposing properly designed logos and gravatars for different media that brand your business, commenting on blogs and forums, and hosting your own blog where customers get educated about your business while building your business as a trusted resource for solving your customer's problems. The cool thing about most new school marketing tools is that most are free.

Gary Vaynerchuk is a successful author, successful business person and a dreamer. He also wants to own the New York Jets and has a mouth like a drunken sailor. Something remarkable Gary has done is he has bridged old school marketing with new school marketing. I had the pleasure of interviewing Gary after he gave a talk promoting his book The Thank You Economy at Kepler's Books in Menlo Park, CA. Besides sharing the insights in his book, Gary told how he took his family-owned wine business and turbo-charged its growth using social media.

Figuratively speaking, successful sales people, have BIG BALLS. It doesn't matter if they're male or female. They have confidence in themselves and their company's product/service and they know their job is to close sales by asking people for their money. They measure their success by how many deals they close and how much money they are making. They use the tools created by the marketing staff, qualify prospects, interact with potential customers, and ask for money. If they go nowhere with clients, they drop them and look for the next wallet. They ask people to sign contracts where money will exchange hands. They are cashiers at stores and restaurants asking for a customer's debit or credit card or cash to finish a transaction. There are even shopping carts on websites that have a submit button which transfers money to their business account. Successful sales people understand their role is to get people through the sales funnel as fast as possible and collect the mighty greenback. They have BIG BALLS.

The relationship between marketing and sales is much like a relay race. Marketing gets things kicked off out of the starting gate. Marketers have an arsenal of branding materials strategically placed to inform potential customers about their business and its product(s). If they do their job right, prospects and leads enter the top of the sales funnel where the baton is passed to the sales department. If you have the right people in the sales department, they can't wait for the baton to be passed to them. They salivate at the lips as their eyes spin around in their eye sockets like a slot machine in Las Vegas. They see the opportunity to make money, grab the baton, and haul ass to close deals.

For those of you who are a one man/woman band business or a small business you're probably wearing a baseball cap with at least two bills. One says marketing and one says sales. If you don't understand the difference between marketing and sales and if you're not willing to promote your business or if you're not willing to ask people for their money, you're probably not fit to be a successful business owner. Almost every successful business owner I have known did not initially feel comfortable with his marketing and sales roles. He/she felt nervous, didn't sleep well, didn't know what to do and wasn't a good public speaker. The great thing is that most marketing and sales skills can be developed and honed with time. There are tons of books, CD's and pod casts that can help you out. I listen to and/or read 3-4 books per month to keep me updated and motivated with my marketing and sales skills. If you haven't read the *chapter Visibility, Credibility, Convertibility, Profitability: If You Don't Have …………. "ibility"…… Don't Open Your Own Business,* you should after reading this chapter.

Take Away: Marketing is the most important task of any business being successful. Simply put, without marketing your business is invisible to people with money. Every successful business has a BIG MOUTH on their staff who likes to hang out with his best buddy who has BIG BALLS

Lustful Lovers Start at First Base, Marketers Start at Second Base: Primary vs. Secondary Market Research

I can remember the first time I ever kissed a girl who wasn't my grandmother or mother. It was winter time and in the basement of Mike DeVincent's house my sophomore year in high school. I had to be the biggest, most naive dork when it came to teenage love. In fact, I was so clueless about teenage love that I didn't even know that the girl sitting next to me in Miss Comeau's English class was flirting with me for the past 3-4 months. The first time I kissed my girlfriend I think it was about as sexy as a 2 year old sitting in a car seat in his mother's minivan plastering their Gerber Baby Food covered lips against the side window slobbering like a scared pig. Yep, that was me, a scared 15 year old who didn't know a French kiss form a Hershey kiss. I sucked at kissing, but somehow I was able to get the grasp with some practice with my girlfriend and from the stupid advice of my two buddies, David Fitzpatrick and Steve Casey. So there you go, it's out in the open, and now all my high school classmates know I never got to first base until that magical winter night my sophomore year in high school.

This chapter is not about my teenage love life or a guide for seducing women. However, I do suggest that when it comes to business market research you skip first base and start on second base. If you're thinking you might get slapped upside the head, remember this chapter is about business market research and not about dating or rekindling an old love affair at your high school reunion.

Why start at second base? Second base, or Secondary Market Research is the use of existing data to study a business opportunity or strategy. If you want to know how many people live in Palo Alto go to Google and type in "how many people live in Palo Alto". You wouldn't go start knocking on doors taking your own census. This is using Secondary Market Research - stuff that already exists that is usually just a few key strokes away.

Primary Market Research is research that you initiate and find and don't borrow or steal from someone else. Politicians use it all the time. They call people and ask them what they think about a hot issue. Smart hopeful small business owners might go to the shopping center and hand out a poll asking mothers if they have kids and if they would like to answer a one minute questionnaire in exchange for a $2.00 Starbucks card. This is primary market research - research where you craft the research techniques and collate the information yourself. Primary Market research usually takes longer than Secondary Market Research to collect and usually costs more money.

If your business already has competitors, use Secondary Market Research to learn about their business. Everyone knows about Google searches for information. If you're in the retail, personal health care and fitness, or restaurant/bar markets Yelp is the fastest way to get a grip on your competitor's product or even how many similar businesses already exist in a given geographic area. By searching on Facebook, you can also learn a lot about your competitors business. Just the fact that they have or don't have a Facebook business page can tell you a lot about how they interact or fail to interact with their customers. Another place to check on businesses and business people is on LinkedIn.

Businesses are able to create a business page on LinkedIn and can even create separate sub-pages for each product or service they offer.

Curious to know what key words your competitors are using to get traffic to their blog or website? Try Google Analytics or Alexa - both sites have lots of info on the keywords used popularly on the web and what your competitors are using.

Finally the last place to put a lot of weight on Primary Market research is your family and friends. Your friends and family will most probably lie to you. Hey, you're not out asking people to be nice to you. This is about your financial future. Family and friends will often hide their true thoughts about your product or service, especially about the not-so-good parts. I would much rather have a stranger tell me my idea sucks and that they wouldn't buy it in a million years than to hear my neighbor say "sounds like a great product" who then later goes home and pees in his pants while laughing his ass off while describing my dumb ass idea to his wife and kids.

Take Away: Use Secondary Market Research before conducting Primary Market Research. Marketers start at second base and lovers start at first base. In case you didn't notice, I never mentioned my high school girlfriend's name. I never kiss and tell.

50 Shades of Brown - The Chicasians are coming! Know Your Demographics and Psychographics

The mother of my children and I have a long standing joke that our kids are "Chicasians." Our kids are half Chicano (of Mexican ancestry on their mother's side) and half Caucasian (Irish and Czech on my side). Chicano + Caucasean = Chicasean. My kid's mother is *morena*. A *morena* is a hispanic female person with light brown skin and a *moreno* is a hispanic male with light brown skin. When our kids go out in the summer sun to go surfing they look like they've magically changed races in just a few hours - they become *morenos* like their mother.

I have two brothers whose wives are of Chinese decent; and one sister whose husband is from Kuala Lampur and is of Indian decent. I also have a niece who is half Dutch-Malai and a sister-in-law who is Cuban-American. When we all get together, it looks like the United Nations decided to hold a pot luck dinner and give a glimpse of what is happening in the United States. The United States population is turning 50 Shades of Brown.

The *Chicasians*, the *Chincaseans*, the *Indiaceans*, the *Afrocaseans* and any other combo of 50 Shades of Brown that you can think of is storming America. I think in the next 20 years, if not sooner, the population of America will be more light brown than white. As a business owner, this trend is too big to ignore. The 50 Shades of Brown America is changing

American politics, restaurant menus, public school foreign language immersion programs, and how home owners talk to their gardeners, dry cleaners and their in-laws. Americans no longer celebrate just Christmas, New Years, Saint Patty's Day or Easter; they celebrate *Noche Buena*, Chinese New Year (CNY), *Dewali*, Indigenous People's Day, *Cinco de Mayo* and *Kwamzaa*. The smorgasbord of Holidays in the U.S. is like a mirror reflecting the many shades of America's people, its cultures and even its business opportunities.

Just as there are democrats and psychopaths, there are demographic and psychographic profiles of people. Demographics deals with classifying people using variables such as age, sex, level of education, racial or ethnic background and the geographic location of people. A quick demographic profile of Palo Alto, CA that I found on the U.S. Census Bureau website for the most recent years tells me there are 65,412 people living in the city; that the population is 64% white, 27% Asian, 6% Hispanic and 3% other races; that 79% of the population over 25 years old has at least a bachelor's degree; that 39% of the households speak a language other than English at home; that the median home costs $1,000,001 and that the median household income is $122,532.00.

For my business, The Kitchen and Bath Company of Palo Alto, I used demographics to focus my marketing efforts even further. Knowing I hate to drive around Social Media Alley and Silicon Valley and that I love to spend time with my family, time exercising, time coaching youth sports and volunteering at my kid's schools - I thought to myself, *"Why not target my business to one of the most affluent areas in Palo Alto that is literally 2-5 minutes from my home?"*

What I did next was go to Google and type in "property values of homes in Palo Alto by neighborhood." I found out that according to the website Zillow, the neighborhood Old Palo Alto has a median home value is $2,556,600. Not $255,660, that's right $2,556,600. Old Palo Alto is home to Steve Jobs' family, one of the founders of Google, many venture capitalists and CEOs and there are even a couple hundred doctors and lawyers who happened to sneak in. The other cool thing about the neighborhood is the majority of the houses are 60-80 years old. I'm not the smartest person in the world, but I do know that if you're in the business of kitchen and bath remodeling, Old Palo Alto may be ground zero for a business that specializes in providing kitchens and baths to home owners whose homes are falling apart, who are over-worked, are highly educated, have large incomes and who don't want to screw around at Home Depot on their weekends.

Psychographics classifies people using variables such as their attitudes and values of a given group of people. Finding psychographic information for your business may be hard to find. For example, when I went to Google and typed in "psychographics for Palo Alto" the first response I got had to do with who makes the best burrito in Menlo Park, CA. Huh? The poll was taken by a total of nine people and according to the poll, Cafe de Sol makes the best burrito. Before I continue, I feel compelled to give a BIG SHOUT OUT to Miss, Mrs., or Mr. algorithm writer at Google – Boy, that search was really helpful! I guess if you're interested in starting a business in Palo Alto the most important thing you need to know is that according to nine people the best place to get a burrito is in Menlo Park. FYI, before conducting this Google Search I'd never eaten at, or heard of, Cafe de Sol.

When I need data for my business and can't find it on the web, I do two things. First, I look and see what consumers are doing and buying; and second, I read between the lines in the local newspapers. Back to my old Palo Alto neighborhood story... Old Palo Alto is full of hybrid Prii (yes that's the plural of Prius), SUVs and electric Tesla sports cars.

Everything I have read tells me that only well-to-do, environmentally-minded people buy expensive hybrid and electric cars. Hmmm, I wonder if my target market wants an environmentally friendly remodel? Green materials, energy efficient appliances and lighting, countertops made from recycled materials, bamboo floors and paints that don't destroy the ozone - most of these materials are important to my Old Palo Alto target market.

Besides being home to Stanford University, Palo Alto must be home to the densest concentration of tutoring businesses in the world. If you need to get tutored in English, Spanish, Chinese, for the PSAT, SAT, LSAT, GMAT, or on how to write a kindergarten or college entrance essay -- Palo Alto must be home to the Tutoring Nirvana Gods. There are tutoring places all over the place. Obviously, your average Palo Altan values education. Educated people tend to make more money than uneducated people and educated people tend to analyze things more than uneducated people. Hmmm, maybe I'll start a class called *"How to Manage Your Kitchen or Bath Remodel Like a Pro"* and teach it at the Palo Alto Adult Education School to gain market exposure. Hmmm, maybe I'll prepare detailed line item budgets for my prospective client's remodels and share it with them. Hmmm, sharing information to help highly educated people make good remodeling decisions will probably help grow my business.

University Avenue in Palo Alto goes from Highway 101 through downtown Palo Alto and leads directly to Memorial Church at Stanford. Downtown Palo Alto is home to some of the nation's most expensive rents and is inundated with restaurants, start-ups and the offices of some of the richest people on planet earth. People who eat out a lot have a high disposable income and are busy. Hmmmm, I don't think these are do-it-yourself home remodelers - in their free time they'd rather be driving golf balls at the Palo Alto Country Club, spending time at their Lake Tahoe cabin, or exercising at Exodus, one of Palo Alto's many health clubs. I don't need more information to validate my business is in a great location. Lots of well educated, wealthy people with super high incomes, living in expensive older homes in need of repair. Thank you, construction Gods for introducing me to Palo Alto during my sophomore year in college.

Knowing how to read between the lines of the local newspaper is something small business owners need to know how to do. In my local papers The Daily Post, The Palo Alto Weekly and The Daily News, I recently saw the following content: an ad by Ken Deleon (the nation's number one realtor in 2012) announcing Kim Heng as his Chinese market marketing expert -- sounds like a lot of Chinese people must be buying homes in Palo Alto. I also read an article where Pollack Financial is trying to get a property re-zoned so that they can build a bigger, non-conforming building at the corner of El Camino Real and Page Mill Road - sounds like the traffic will be getting even worse in Palo Alto and more people will be using Old Palo Alto as a shortcut to get around the already horrible traffic on Page Mill Road. I saw two ads by a company that sells rare coins and gold - sounds like wealthy Palo Altans are looking for different places to diversify their wealth. There's an ad by Stanford Financial

Credit Union offering Home Equity Lines of Credit - sounds like property values are rising in Palo Alto.

Having the ability to scan and read between the lines of different local papers allows me to summarize what's going on in Palo Alto and how it will affect my kitchen and bath business. In sum, it sure looks like more Chinese people are moving to Palo Alto and that many current home owners are using home equity lines of credit to either improve their homes or make investments.

Take Away: It's important to know the demographics and psychographics of your business' target market. With the help of Google, some local newspapers, and a drive around town, you may be able to get all the info you need to validate your business idea. When you're done reading 50 Shades of Grey spend some time understanding the 50 Shades of Brown that impact your business; and if you're looking for psychographic information on your business in Palo Alto, don't waste your time using Google unless you're in Menlo Park and hungry for a burrito.

Don't be a Sponge Bob - Convert Prospects to Paying Clients Quickly

I don't know how many times I've heard small business owners tell me that their business is doing well and that they're working with lots of potential clients. I've also seen these same business owners flounder financially as they spend lots of time with potential clients who in the end never gave the biz owner a dime. What the heck is going on here and why? These business owners have been soaked of their time and in most cases have given away their expertise for free. These business owners are Sponge Bobs.

Here's a true story about me. For years, I have worked in Palo Alto, CA as a General Contractor remodeling homes. For many years, I would meet with potential clients at all times of the day and on any day of the week. My health suffered from lack of sleep and lack of exercise and my family suffered by me allowing these meetings to eat into my family time. One day, I was talking with a good friend of mine Iris who is also a successful contractor. Iris told me she doesn't meet with potential clients at any old time that is convenient for the potential client and on top of that she charges to do estimates. At first, I couldn't believe what she was saying. She told me that she takes care of her own health before her client's scheduling problems and that by charging to do estimates, she qualifies customers before they sponge away her time and knowledge and never become a customer. She qualifies people quickly and converts them to paying customers quickly. If they don't qualify, she's off looking for people who do qualify. What happened next? After talking with Iris, I had my epiphany and changed my way of thinking. I vowed to never be a Business Sponge Bob again.

If you're not in a business that collects money immediately like a coffee shop, hair salon, restaurant, bar, copy center or dry cleaner, you run the risk of people sponging away your time and expertise. You're a possible Sponge Bob. The key is to get these people from being prospects to paying customers as fast as possible. Lawyers ask for retainers, web designers ask for a deposit, realtors ask for sellers to sign a listing agreement, and successful contractors ask for a deposit to make a detailed analysis of the home owner's potential project. Successful business owners know the value of their services, know how to market their services, understand that sales involve putting your balls on the table and asking for money and refusing to be a Sponge Bob.

So how do you qualify potential customers quickly and lock them into being paying customers? If at all possible, you qualify them before you meet them belly button to belly button. Make a list of questions that you would ask the potential client that qualifies them by finding out their needs, what their objections are, and if you should spend any time with them. If possible, you qualify potential customers by using the phone or your web page. If you're a lawyer, you find out what the potential client's problem is, find out if you can help them and then let them know you charge $300/hour to help them out. If you're a web designer, you find out what the potential client wants built, have them look at your portfolio on your website and then schedule a meeting where the potential client is instructed to bring their checkbook. If you're a realtor, you find out why the potential client needs to sell their home, you make sure all the decision makers will be at the meeting, and you ask them that if you're able to meet their needs will they be willing to sign a listing agreement at your meeting. If you're a successful contractor, you find out when and why the home owner wants to remodel their home, where the home is located, how they heard about you, and then let them know you will be willing to look at the project, and finally that you charge for your time after the first meeting.

Take Away: Understand that potential clients are not paying customers that allow you to make money. Many potential customers have no interest in buying from you or they don't have the financial resources to hire you. These are the users in life – the people that will give you the impression they are going to be your customer when in reality all there doing is stealing your time and expertise. As a business owner, you need to have a system in place to qualify potential customers as quick as possible and convert them to paying customers. If you don't follow the advice in this chapter, please send me an e-mail so I can send you your invitation to the Sponge Bob Club.

What You can learn from Your Neighborhood Crack Dealer: Freemium to Premium

First let's get if off the table -- I've never tried crack. However, I knew a crack dealer when I worked in Costa Rica. And just in case you've heard any rumors about my earlier partying days when I was in college, yes I got thrown out of a Sheraton Hotel in San Diego for dancing on the table tops.

Anyway, back to my crack dealer story in Costa Rica and what it means to your business. Quepos, Costa Rica is home to Manuel Antonio Park, Costa Rica's most famous national park, and is also home to some of the world's best surfing and sport fishing and has casinos and a great night life. In short, Quepos is a tourist magnet and is full of people looking for a good time. Giovanni was one of the many local drug dealers and scammers in Quepos. Every time my path crossed with Giovanni's he would suggest that today was a great day for me to sample some of his FREE CRACK. I never took Giovanni up on his offer but I did learn something from him about drug dealers and smart business owners.

A great way to get someone to try your product or service is to initially offer your product or service for free or to give them a scaled down version of your product for free and then to later charge them for the continued use of the product or charge for a better version of the product with added features. Start'm free, hook'm, and then charge'm once they can't live without your product or service just like Giovanni was trying to do with me. Freemium to Premium. I'm not suggesting anyone become a drug dealer; however I am suggesting you should take a good look at your business and see if Freemium to Premium might help your business grow.

Freemium to Premium has become the norm for many old school businesses and for most online businesses nowadays. Classic examples are: a software company letting you use its software for free for 30 days; LinkedIn having a scaled down version of its membership with an enhanced product you pay for; a dance studio offers the first class for free; Web Lunch Box offers a free social media training class to a group of small business owners; an online store offers a free book or audio recording to sample their product; a company like Vertical Response offers a free real estate listing product but has a better version that you can pay for – the list goes on and on. All these businesses know that the odds of getting new paying customers are better if you offer them something for free and then to switch them to a paying customer once they've proved their product or service works and they've had time to build trust with the potential customer.

Take Away: Giving something away for free (if you haven't read the chapter *Want to Make Money? Try Giving Something Away for Free!,* read it next) may be the first step to creating a profitable business using the Freemium to Premium model and if you're ever in Quepos, Costa Rica and meet a friendly "tico" named Giovanni who is overly gracious and friendly I suggest you grab your surfboard and fishing pole and run away as fast as you can.

Want to Make Money? Try Giving Something Away Free!

After the word sex, the word free (no, I didn't say free sex) is probably the biggest attention-catcher word you can use to get someone's attention. Consumers have become accustomed to getting something for free as business owners try and build a relationship with potential purchasers of their product or service. We're all accustomed to free samples at Costco, the local coffee shop or bakery, free perfume samples at Nordstrom's or Macy's and free shipping with our online purchases from Amazon.com or L.L. Bean.

Is free really free? And are all businesses benevolent entities truly giving away free stuff at the expense of their company's bottom line? If you believe this to be true, here's a smack upside your head to knock some common sense in to you. Free offers serve two roles: first, to start the relationship building process between a business and its potential customers; and secondly, to get you to do business with their business instead of their competitors. Web Lunch Box and HubSpot (a pioneer in inbound marketing tools) are two businesses that get this idea loud and clear. If your business doesn't adapt to this concept quickly, it's likely to get run over by the competition. So how does Web Lunch Box and HubSpot use "free" to modify potential customer's behavior? Simple. Both offer free e-books and free social media classes to start the relationship building process. Once people receive something for free they're much more likely to give you their contact info and to make a purchase from you. The key thing to remember here is that "free" starts building a relationship between a business and its customers and adds perceived value to the customer.

Does Amazon.com and LLBean.com really offer free shipping? Of course not. Both companies have built in to their pricing model the cost of the shipping into the price of their products. Here's the funny thing I just saw while writing this chapter. Zappos.com an online shoe store, offers free shipping both ways on your purchase. In other words, if you need to return the product they'll pick up the cost of shipping back to the Zappos warehouse. And do Costco, Nordstorm's, Macy's and Starbucks give free stuff away? Believe me someone has studied consumer behavior and knows that by giving "free samples" their bottom line is bigger due to increased sales.

Old school free still has its place in the small business world. When I was in my early twenties, I used to paint houses with my brother Michael to help pay for our college education. Our parents raised Michael and me to have integrity and to understand the meaning of hard work in exchange for money. The only problem Michael and I had was that we looked like we were 14 and 16 years old and nobody believed we were mature enough to paint their houses. So what did we do? We went around the Midtown area of Palo Alto putting up fliers at the local stores, put them on car windshields and went door to door introducing ourselves and we used the power of free. Our sales proposition was simple: let us paint your house with no down payment for our services and pay us when we're done. If you're not happy with our work don't pay us - our services are FREE if you're not happy. People in Midtown, Palo Alto soon learned we knew what we were doing and referred us to their friends and told them about our 100% happiness guarantee or the work was free. FYI, we NEVER didn't get paid.

To this day, I still know the value of free and let the customers of Web Lunch Box know that if they're not 100% satisfied with our services, we will refund their money no questions asked. Since Web Lunch Box' inception, only one person has asked for their money to be refunded and this person had to withdraw from a class I was teaching. HubSpot's twist on this model is they let you try their software free for a limited time before making a cash purchase. If you don't like their software there's zero financial risk to you.

Don't be late - Differentiate, Create and innovate and don't Drive a White Ford F150

Have you ever seen a school bus that isn't painted yellow? I don't think I have ever seen a school bus painted any color except yellow. Have you ever wondered why most fire trucks and ambulances are painted red? Why is this? It's simple. Public safety officials have learned that yellow school buses and red fire trucks and ambulances are easier to see than any other colored vehicles. They are easy to differentiate from the other vehicles and they stand out in a crowd.

Now, in the same way you should ask yourself. Is your business easy to differentiate from your competitors? Does it stand out in a crowd? Most building contractors drive white pick-up trucks and most contractors don't put signs on their vehicles. Why is this? Believe it or not, white trucks don't show road dirt and grime as much as darker vehicles. Why not have trucks I don't have to wash and why not go watch the 49ers instead of putting a sign on my truck? Is this good business? I don't think so. For my construction company, I drive a bright yellow van and put reflective yellow signs that are made from the same type of material that stops signs are made from. My truck stands out in a crowd and is easy to differentiate from other contractors trucks. When its dark out and the headlights of passing cars flash on my truck, it lights up like the signals at a train crossing. Even though I only drive around Palo Alto in my van and Chevy Suburban I've had many people ask me how many vehicles I own because they have seen my fleet of trucks driving around Palo Alto.

The ability to think differently, to be creative, to think outside the box, to innovate by changing an existing paradigm can be a trump card when it comes to tilting the playing field to your advantage. Gino Blefari, the CEO and Founder of Intero Real Estate Services, is one of the most creative businessmen I've worked with. When Gino first started Intero, he had an idea that seems so simple but it rocked the local real estate market and pissed off a lot of complacent realtors.

We're all used to seeing real estate agents planting "For Sale" signs in their client's front yard. In fact, I don't know a single agent who doesn't do it. Gino looked at the signage model and flipped it on its head. When it comes to selling one's home, aren't sellers really most interested in who are the agents that can bring buyers who are able and willing to buy the seller's home? You bet they are. So Gino did something radically different to let home owners near the house that just sold, know that he brought the buyer. How? Gino looked at something as old as the mouse trap, put on his creative thinking cap and came up with a new innovation. He called it "The Buyer's Representation Sign." After the transaction closed and the listing agent had removed the sold sign, Gino puts up his own sign -The Buyer's Representation Sign. What the heck is a Buyers Representation Sign? It's an Intero sign letting everyone in the neighborhood know he knew how to find buyers. After planting the Buyer's Representation sign in the front yard, Gino then gets his happy new home owner to write a great testimonial of his work, makes copies of it, and distributes it to all the neighbors. No wonder Intero is one of the fastest growing real estate companies in the United States.

Take Away: Most business owners are lazy or too busy spending time on things that don't help bring in customers to grow their business. When it comes to differentiating your business from your competitors, first

implement the time proven tools that work. Second, be creative and innovative, put a new spin on something old, and use it to your advantage. If you're lazy or under-funded and don't promote your business in the most basic ways, you will get run over by someone who catches you sleeping at the wheel.

You Might Not be Square, But Your Logo Should Be: Tips for Designing Your Company Logo

I feel sorry for most graphic designers who are in the logo design business. Graphic artists were once paid hundreds, if not thousands of dollars, to design company logos and were treated like gods as they instructed business owners under no circumstances were they to screw with their company logo. Logos were holier than the Bible and cut in stone. It's as if logo designers were rich parents instructing their children that if they screwed with their logo they would be cut out of the family inheritance. Logo design has experienced a lobotomy in the last ten years. Need a logo and don't have a lot of money? Now you can find someone on oDesk.com or eLance.com who will gladly design your logo and give you three different concepts and three different revisions of their work all for $50.

If you don't believe me about the sanctity of business logos, just look at Google. Google is the most sacrilegious murderer of logos as it gets. Every day when I log in to my computer, I'm interested to see what bizarre or funny thing Google has done to its logo on their search page. I don't think I've ever seen Google not change their logo on their search page. When it comes to designing your company logo, you don't have to be as loose as Google but you should look at having at least two, if not three, different designs made that you will use on a daily basis.

The first version of your logo I recommend you look at making is a square version of your logo for mobile phones, for your Twitter thumbnail and for your company *gravatar*. Turn on any smart phone or log in to Twitter and you'll see only square shaped logos, better known as thumbnails, on the main menu screen. There are no rectangular, circular or other shaped logos - only square shapes with rounded edges. In case you're wondering what a *gravatar* is it is stands for "globally recognized avatar" which really stands for the image you use when you comment on other peoples blogs *(see You've Seen The Movie Avatar; But Where's Your Gravatar?)* If you don't have a square shaped version of your logo, under certain circumstances your logo will automatically get truncated and just look shit%y.

The second version of your logo you will most likely want is a rectangular logo with a long horizontal axis. This is the Google original logo format. Why a logo with a long horizontal axis? It looks good on most company letterheads, looks good on most social media sites and fills out the header of your company blog nicely. With this format you have much more leeway than the square version of your logo wherein you can add a tag line, address, contact info, website address or perhaps a picture of yourself.

The third version of your logo you may want to have designed is a rectangular logo with a long vertical axis. In the past I've seen this format used a lot on Facebook where the business wishes to include their contact info at the top of their Facebook profile. By designing a logo with a long vertical axis and incorporating contact information in the logo there is no need for the person visiting the profile to scroll down or search for contact info.

Another thing to consider when designing your company logo is considering what it looks like in black and white and when printed on a copying machine or fax machine. Some logos, especially dark logos using different shades of color may look great on a computer screen, but when printed out in black and white may be illegible or be unrecognizable.

Take Away: Your company logo will be viewed on smart phones, laptops, tablets and desktop and websites, blogs, Facebook, Twitter and mobile apps. For most businesses, it has become important to have a square and rectangular version of their logo. Also, if you or one of your kids is thinking of becoming a logo designer take a hard look at the business model to see if it's something you can live off.

Band U2, Brand U Too - Be ""Younique"""

Anyone who is a fan of Rock 'n Roll for the last 30 years knows the band U2. It doesn't matter if you like U2's music; one sound from The Edge's guitar or the first note from Bono's voice and you know its U2. Their sound is unique and hypnotic and the subject of many of their songs has to do with social justice and peace. Unique sound, unique songs. U2 is unique.

Own your own business? Be ""Younique"".... What can you do to distinguish your business from the sea of competition? What are you passionate about? What are you doing to make the world a better place? How can you share your ""Younique"" characteristics that distinguish you from your competition?

Tim Helion is one of my high school classmates (Dover Sherborn Regional High School, Dover, Massachusetts, Class of 1977) who now lives in Reno, Nevada. Tim is a friendly man who wears his heart and soul on the sleeve of his shirt. Tim is also passionate about bicycle riding. He also has a BIG NOSE. As in literally, a big nose. Tim knows it and he's proud of it. So when Tim decided to open a coffee shop with one of his friends who also has a big nose, together they decided to name their coffee shop *Deux Gros Nez*– which means The Two Big Noses in French.

Is there something *"Younique"* about you that you can bring to your business? In my case, my last name is spelled Hmelar with the H being silent – thus, my last name is pronounced Mil-lar.

Hmelar in Czech means "hops" - like the hops they use to make beer. People may not

remember the correct spelling of my last name but they know enough that when they try to find me on Facebook or on LinkedIn they don't have to look too hard.

Ask yourself. What are the things you are passionate about that your customers can connect with? What can you do that will brand you and your business as having a *"Younique"* twist? Ken Delion was the United States number one realtor for the year 2012 and he also happens to live in the same town as I. He is constantly placing *"Younique"* ads in the local papers with what seem to be "off-the-wall" advertisements, describing himself as a creative and savvy realtor who thinks outside the box. Ken even brings a full espresso bar, deli and band to his client's open houses. These are *"Younique"* tactics for promoting himself and he sure knows how to get clients. Last year Ken sold over 300 million dollars of real estate. Now, that's how far being *"Younique"* will take you.

Take Away: It can pay big time to be *"Younique"*. Spend some time trying to think of how you can brand your business as being *"Younique"*. Be proud of your *"Younique*ness" and let your customers know about it. If you're not sure how to get started and you need some help getting your creative juices flowing to find your *"Younique*ness", I suggest you pop on your iPod, listen to some U2 music, put on some Groucho Marx glasses and go for a bike ride around Palo Alto. Who knows maybe you'll bump into Tim Helion on his bike or stop by one of Ken Delion's open houses and score a free lunch.

Biz Strategy

Jon Bon Jovi Writes More than Rock 'n' Roll Hits, He Knows How to Write a Biz Plan

Jon Bon Jovi is one of Rock 'n' Roll's greatest musicians and entertainers. He's also a great businessman, sports team owner, and philanthropist and even has a country music hit. Just as Bon Jovi knows how to use a pen to write number one hits, he also knows the power of writing down one's dreams and writing a business plan to make those dreams a reality.

"Map out your future - but do it in pencil. The road ahead is as long as you make it. Make it worth the trip." - Jon Bon Jovi

Colin Kaepernick, a San Francisco Fourty Niners quarterback, wrote a letter to himself when he was just 9 years old and in the fourth grade. In the letter he wrote how he was a good athlete, wanted to go to a good college and hoped to play for the Fourty Niners or Green Bay Packers when he got older. The funny thing is that it all happened.

Gino Blefari, a personal friend of mine, is the Founder and CEO of Intero Real Estate Services headquartered in Cupertino, CA. Intero has grown to be one of the nation's top real estate firms in just 10 years and is already expanding internationally. Every October, Gino updates his personal/business plan. I've personally read Gino's business plan and he leaves nothing to chance. Everything Gino wants to see happen with Intero, he visualizes first and then puts it down on paper. Gino so strongly believes in the power of writing down one's business plan that he e-mails every Intero agent a business plan template every October and coaches the agents to fill it out so that his agent's have a written business plan to guide them to their business success. While most real estate agents start to "slack off" at the Fall holiday season, Gino coaches his agents to "grow for it" and go out, and kick ass and take names while the competitors get lazy and complacent during the holidays. No wonder many of Intero's agents routinely have their best sales months while others are off eating turkey, celebrating December's holidays with eggnog or are out nursing their New Year's Eve hangover.

So what's the big deal about writing down ones goals and writing a business plan? Not only does writing a business plan allow you to flush out business ideas, marketing plans, budget forecasts and help you raise money; writing down your business plan re-wires your brain. It changes the way your brain thinks and what it focuses on. Writing down your business plan changes the neurological pathways in your brain. Your brain will literally be re-wired and start to think differently. When you take an idea that you think about and then write it down your brain changes and says to itself *"Hey I'm supposed to make this happen. This person isn't playing; this is serious so hop on it and let's make this happen."*

Take Away: Jon Bon Jovi, Colin Kaepernick and Gino Blefari didn't get to the top of their respective fields by chance. They work incredibly hard at their craft and write important things down. They have a written plan to guide them to their success. If you want your business dream to become a reality, I suggest you get inspired by turning on Bon Jovi's song *Living on a Prayer*, write out your business plan and start re-wiring your brain for success.

Proper, Prior, Planning, Prevents, Post, Poor, Performance: The 7 P's of Pre-Planning Business Success

The first time I was introduced to "Proper, Prior, Planning, Prevents, Post, Poor, Performance", it was being explained to me by my friend David Fitzpatrick's father. David and I were sharing with Mr. Fitzpatrick our half-baked plan to go to Cape Cod for the weekend. Our plan, if you call it a plan, was not planned out at all. We didn't know how we were going to get to the Cape, where we we're going to stay, or how we were going to finance our trip. It was at this moment, and I remember this like it was yesterday, Mr. Fitzpatrick said "Proper, Prior, Planning, Prevents, Post, Poor, Performance. It's obvious you two don't have a plan, and no, you're not going to the Cape."

 The key concept of the 7 P's of Pre-planning for Business Success is that successful people take the time to prepare for something before that event happens (whether the event is predictable or not).   It doesn't matter whether you're planning a trip to Cape Cod, you're a professional athlete, someone trying to get a better job, someone trying to meet a possible mate or someone trying to grow their business -- being prepared in advance is vital. If you don't take the time and effort for advanced preparation, there is a good chance that your competition will have crossed paths with someone like Mr. Fitzpatrick, will have learned the 7 P's lesson and will kick you in the butt. The professional athlete, take Jerry Rice or Steve Young, dominates in his sport by putting in extra training above and beyond his teammates; the student who finishes college or networks with influential business people gets the better job; the lonely person looking for a mate dresses to kill attracting a would be mate; and the successful business owner plans out all the steps to tilt the playing field to his/her advantage.

For the past year I've had the goal of interviewing and recording the world's top social media experts. Part of my strategy and preparation for this goal is to always carry two camcorders and a great 35 MM camera with me everywhere I go. Guy Kawasaki, a bestselling author, successful biz person, thought leader and nice guy was on my list of people to interview. I swear, just yesterday, I was preparing to give a presentation on Facebook Business Pages at Kepler's Books and Magazines in Menlo Park, CA when who goes walking by me? That's right, Guy Kawasaki. Guy was at Kepler's to autograph some books. I quickly grabbed my camera bag, approached Guy, introduced myself, let him know what I was up to and asked him if I could interview him. Guy smiled at me and agreed to let me interview him. Fifteen minutes later I had my interview and a personally autographed copy of Guy Kawasaki's latest book *Enchanted*.

Take Away: See Mr. Fitzpatrick, I did learn the 7 P's.

Visibility, Credibility, Convertibility, Profitability: If you don't Have ......"ibility" ...... Don't Open Your Business

Having a great idea, money to fund your start-up, and lots of ambition does not ensure biz success. If you don't know how to market your business, close a sale and charge properly, there's a good chance you'll waste time, lose money, maybe lose your family and your biz will fail. For your biz to succeed, you must understand the 4 "ilities": Visibility, Credibility, Convertibility and Profitability.

Visibility: To put it simply, if people don't know your business exists you won't get customers. Sounds stupid, but I know many businesses that have no web presence, no biz card, have opened stores with no signage, work in construction, and don't put up a job sign in the front yard to name just a few. You must have a plan to get your name out there. The triple punch I use for marketing my business services are old school networking, creating happy customers who refer my biz, and using social media.

Credibility: If you don't know what you're doing in business look out. Not only will people discover you don't know what you're doing, they will let everyone know that you're fake, that you don't deliver, and if you really screw someone over you may find yourself in court. There is more to building credibility for your business than simply delivering on your business promise. Yes, it's true you need to do what you say you are going to do (see the *5 E's of Business*), in the time frame and at the price you promise, yet you must do more if you really want your business to thrive. Become an expert on your biz niche and let others know about it. A good friend of mine, Iris Harrell of Harrell Remodeling in Mountain View, CA is a master of marketing her remodeling business. Iris writes for different publications, has won many awards, has served on the board of many construction associations and holds many seminars to educate potential clients on home remodeling. Iris delivers on her construction promises and she lets potential clients she knows what she's doing, in fact, for the construction industry she does it better than anyone else I know.

Convertibility: You or someone on your business team must have the balls to ask for and close the order. This is called sales. The sales process converts prospects to paying clients. I've heard time and time again of businesses owners saying *"I'm working with a client or customer and my business is looking great,"* only to find out three months later that their so called client or customer was really just a prospect sucking my biz friend for knowledge. REMEMBER THIS: A CUSTOMER IS SOMEONE WHO GIVES YOU MONEY. If you don't receive money from a so called customer or client, don't call them a customer or client – they are a prospect and may be playing you as a Sponge Bob sucking you dry of your time and knowledge. In order to survive in business, your marketing efforts of creating visibility and credibility serve no purpose unless you CONVERT leads in to paying customers.

Profitability: Bean counters have a role in every business. In most small businesses, YOU WILL BE THE BEAN COUNTER! You must know what it costs to deliver your product or service and you must build in a profit margin that allows you to make your personal financial goals become a reality. Having a successful marketing and sales program doesn't ensure you will make enough money for you to live a successful life as a biz owner. The bean counting role is your reality check on the financial viability of your business idea. Whenever possible, perform this function BEFORE starting your business and if possible, test your idea by offering your product or service on a limited basis to people who are not your friends or family and ask them to write you checks for the product or service you provide. I strongly suggest you read *The Four Hour Work Week* by Timothy Ferriss. If you can't make the necessary profit for your personal financial goals to come true, don't start your business.

Take Away: If your business doesn't have "ibility" you probably don't have the ability to run a successful business.

Start-ups

Test Your Idea before Flushing Your Family's Money down the Toilet!

Most entrepreneurs and small business owners I know are sick dudes. They seem to have a special kind of blindness that prevents them from seeing anything that might question the validity of their business idea. They may have an innovative iPhone app like Fridge Police that tracks expiration dates of packages in your fridge, maybe they sell jelly fish aquariums and jelly fish like Jelly Fish Art, maybe they plan to build another Mexican restaurant in the same block as an existing Mexican restaurant, maybe they have a new franchise idea that paints parking spaces in parking lots like We Do Lines (sounds like a bunch of coke fiends to me). The list goes on and on. The one thing they seem to have in common is a type of cataract on their eyes that prevents them from seeing things rationally. Sometimes their ideas work, but most times they fail.

I'm convinced the gnome mapping project will eventually identify a gene called the entrepreneur's overly optimistic attitude gene. This gene will be present in 100% of the nutcase scientists, dreamers, small business owners and marketers who think they've developed the next greatest and latest product or service. I also believe most of these people will be broke, living in squalor and/or will have some story about how some other nutcase stole their idea. The majority of them will have the same story where they were on the brink of success when they got the knees kicked out from under them. These same people will never look in the mirror and look at themselves and say *"Boy, did I screw up, what was I thinking and what the heck was I smoking?"* The easiest sign of identifying someone with this overly optimistic gene is that they never spent any time doing market research to see if anyone else felt the same about the business idea.   Basic questions like: Would people buy the product or service? How much are they willing to pay for it? How much will it cost to produce this thing? How long will it take to make it? Do I have money to pay my personal bills while I get this biz off the ground?   Nope, these sick dudes tend to jump feet first in to the start-up swimming pool with cement shoes on and wonder why their idea drowned.

The key to finding out if your business idea makes sense is to find out as quickly as possible if there are a sufficient number of customers for your product who are willing and able to buy it while minimizing your time and financial exposure in doing your initial work. If you haven't read my chapter *Lustful Lovers Start at First Base; Marketers Start at Second Base. Primary vs Secondary Market Research,* dog ear tag this page; go read it now and then come back to this page.

Once you've done your market research, some questions you might ask yourself are: Can you build a mock-up of your product with scaled down features, can prospective clients blind test your world famous guacamole and do they all think it's better than the guacamole served at Jack in the Box? Can you build a website for a client at no charge to see if they love it? Can you build a second website and have someone pay you for it? Can you remodel a kitchen or bath and do it on time and on budget? Can you design and set up a custom Facebook page for a small biz owner who raves about it? Does Palo Alto really need another dentist office or SAT prep class school? Can you manage a small business' website SEO and show that you actually increased traffic?

Before you go buy a new computer, a new table saw, or a thousand avocados or before you get business cards printed and rent an office – have you completed your SWOT Analysis, your KSF statement, and calculated the burn rate of your business idea? If you haven't done this, you should read this complete section of this book before starting your business. It'll be worth your 20 minutes of time and may save you a ton of time, money and stress. It may also help you make a fortune.

If you've decided to move forward with your idea, I suggest you test out your product or service on a small group of people for free. The purpose of this test is to get feedback so you can make improvements to your wonder widget and get testimonials from people who love your product. I strongly suggest you NOT skip this step. Releasing your product too early on customers who expect a flawless product will barbeque you on Yelp if they're unhappy. On the other hand, your beta testers know they are guinea pigs and that there will probably be shortcomings in whatever they are testing. They have expectations that are lower than paying customers and they won't go barbeque you on Yelp.

Once you have happy beta testers and have tweaked your product or service, get testimonials from your beta testers. Testimonials can be in the form of written reviews, photos of people using your product, or video testimonials. These testimonials will be used to tell your story to lure paying customers.

Once you've tested the idea, the next step is to get someone to actually pay you for the service or product. The key to testing the idea is to deliver a version of the product to someone who will actually pay you for it.

Take Away:

1. Don't ask friends and family if you have a great idea. Ask strangers who are business owners what they think of your idea instead.

2. If biz owners like the idea, figure out what it will cost to deliver your product or service.

3. Sell a limited sample of your product or service to biz owners.

4. Read The Four Hour Work Week by Timothy Ferriss and check out Tim's thoughts on testing your biz idea.

5. Make sure you have a plan to pay your bills while you start your biz.

Burn Baby Burn - Disco Inferno Start-Ups Burn Personal & Business Money Fast

My teenage years were one of the most schitzo times in the music industry. The year was 1976. I was sixteen years old, a junior in high school living in a small town called Sherborn about 15 miles West of Boston, MA. I remember driving around with my girlfriend Lois in a hot rod Chevelle blasting Aerosmith, Boston and the J. Geils Band and then pushing some buttons radio or on the 8 track player and switching to the likes of the Bee Gees, Donna Summer and some group called the Trammps. The Trammps had a song called Disco Inferno where the chorus was a hypnotic beat repeating *"Burn Baby Burn"*. It was a time when Rock 'n' Roll and Disco were clashing head to head for the youth of America's attention and money. It was a time of long haired freaking looking dudes wearing hand-me-down Viet Nam Army jackets taunting the first metrosexuals dressed in leisure suits. As I look back 35 years later its clear to me that Rock 'n' Roll won as I still hear Aerosmith on the radio. With all the changes that happened since my high school years, I must admit though that I still like Disco Inferno and its lyrics.

Since graduating from high school and moving to Palo Alto, I've become all too familiar with a different kind of chorus singing out *"Burn Baby Burn."* It is the voice of the overly optimistic entrepreneur with the latest and greatest idea that will change the world. It is also usually a voice that underestimates how much time the business will need to get off the ground and how much additional money will be needed as well. The entrepreneur more often than not underestimates the *"Burn Baby Burn"* of both time and money.

When planning a new venture whether it be a high tech company, a restaurant, hair salon or some other new business, you as an owner needs to understand that you are about to become a fire fighter and will be fighting two fires at the same time. The first fire will be managing your personal expenses and the other will be the business expenses sucking away time and money like there's no tomorrow. I don't know how many times I've heard one of the main reason businesses fail is because they are under-capitalized. The business simply doesn't have enough cash to get it off the ground and more often than not the entrepreneur burns through their life savings while destroying their credit rating along the way in an effort to prop up a business that will never fly. Believe me I know, I've been there and done it. It sucks.

Soooooooooooooooooo before you decide to jump in and become a new business owner, you need to make two different budgets. Your first budget should be a personal budget of all your expenses, your mortgage or rent, your food, your utilities, haircuts, kids summer camp, medical expenses, car payment and repairs, all the way to toilet paper. Don't underestimate this budget. If you like to eat out or go to the movies throw that in to your budget too. Your budget should reflect monthly changes. For example if you have property taxes due in the Spring or Fall factor that in to your budget and if your heating or AC bill goes up in certain months you should factor that in as well. Don't forget car registration and any other lump sum payments due sometime during the year. Whatever you do don't underestimate your personal budget.

When preparing your business budget you need to calculate the monthly recurring expenses and the start-up burn. Normally, the monthly recurring expenses are rent, utilities, office supplies, Wifi and phone bills, your assistant's/employee's salary and your web hosting account, etc. The start-up burn is all the stuff you need to get the business off the ground, logo design, website design, office or store build out, signage, product development, legal and accounting fees and all the other junk that sucks away money like a huge Hoover vacuum cleaner before you've made a penny in sales. Your Burn Budget should be calculated for at least each of the next 12 months. Just like your personal budget, don't underestimate the amount you will need to come up with to give your business wings.

I can tell you from personal experience if you don't put realistic personal and business budgets together there are two possible scenarios most likely to happen. You will either dip into your personal line of credit (which may be your mom and dad), maybe even sell a house in an effort to save your business and your pride (which will most likely just delay the inevitable business failure) or you will close your business down a less wealthier person who would have been better off staying home watching Jerry Springer. Either way, not planning to face the *"Burn Baby Burn"* is not a good idea. If you do put your budgets together and have the money to weather the Burn you will have removed one of the biggest obstacles of your business failing.

Take Away: Forecast your Personal and Company's Monthly Budget and start-up Burn statements. Don't skimp on these budgets - if anything while calculating your Start-Up's burn you'd be better off doubling or tripling how much time and/or money will be needed to get things going. If you don't have a plan to handle the time and money burn needed to get your business self-sufficient you may end up a tramp and I don't mean a member of the successful disco band The Trammps.

The 5 E's of Managing a Small Business: From Doughnuts to Divorces

Are you a small business owner wishing to grow your business and obtain more customers? If so, you need to know the 5 E's of managing a small business for your specific business field. It doesn't matter if you're selling doughnuts or dealing with divorces, the rules of the game still applies.

The First E - Expectations: What does your customer expect from engaging in a business relationship with you? It doesn't matter if you are selling doughnuts or divorces. You must know what your customers' expectations are and be able to meet that need. If you can't deliver a great doughnut or end an unhappy marriage - don't offer your services at all.

The Second E - Economics: Can you meet your clients' needs at the agreed upon price? All parties to a business transaction like/need/or want to know what it is going to cost. You might walk into a doughnut shop and buy a doughnut without asking the cost of a doughnut, but it's highly unlikely you would hire a divorce lawyer without knowing the cost of getting divorced.

The Third E - Efficiency: Will you be able to deliver your doughnut or divorce in the fastest and most efficient way possible? You can't waste your time or your customer's time providing your service and you can't spend financial resources for long that makes you lose money. How many people are going to wait more than five minutes for their doughnut or how many people are going to agree to spend more time than necessary with their psycho spouse while you play golf or go on Vacation.

The Fourth E - Effective: Can you deliver on your promise to meet your clients' expectations? If you deliver a bagel instead of a doughnut or spend months of a client's time and money only to deliver a Temporary Restraining Order instead of the desired divorce, you will have unhappy clients. Not only will you have unhappy clients, but worst they will tell everyone they know what an idiot you are when it comes to business. And if they use Yelp they will go out and publicly trash you and your business on the internet.

The Fifth E - Evangelist: Here's the super cool thing. If you meet your customer's expectations, deliver your service at the agreed upon price (economics), do it within the agreed length of time (efficiency), deliver exactly what you agreed upon or beat the agreed upon expectation (effective), you end up with an unpaid marketing and sales Evangelist for your business. You can't beat having a raving fan of your business telling everyone they know about your product or services. And if your customer is on the internet, they might even go to Yelp and publicly tell everyone how great your business is.

Take Away: It is imperative you know all 5 E's of your client base if you plan on running a successful business. If you're married, and haven't identified the 5 E's unique to your business - I suggest you hop on down to your local doughnut and figure this out before starting your business so you don't have to later hop on down the street to your local divorce attorney.

Economics 101 and AK47s: Your SWOT Analysis

My biggest business blunder was trying to set up a real estate company in Mexico 18 months before the U.S. economy drove into a ditch. In addition to the fiscal mess at home, the Mexican drug cartels decided to shoot up Mexico and close down the tourism industry. What at first appeared to be a great business opportunity, turned into a business nightmare. Four years before the United States real estate collapse statistics showed, Americans were buying property in Mexico in droves. Great weather, cheap housing with clean titles, easy transportation to and from Mexico and continued access to medical care in the U.S. was luring thousands of Americans to become real estate investors in our neighbor to the South. It looked like one big unending *Cinco de Mayo* party. Everyone was dancing to the *La Bamba* and sucking down Margaritas and shots of Jose Cuervo. My college economics professors were right! Supply meets demand and consumers do determine the true fair price of products and services. The economic business model of the Mexican real estate market looked great! But then something happened; actually, two things happened. And neither was good for me, my family or my business.

Overnight, millions of Americans watched their net worth and retirements evaporate destroying a lifetime of savings. The mortgage industry and Wall Street had pulled off the biggest financial scam in U.S. history. Mortgages were given to anyone with a heartbeat. House values skyrocketed and everyone was jubilant. Only problem, the ecstatic real estate love festival was more like a bunch of ecstatic teenagers on ecstasy at a rave rather than a group of sound investors attending a Donald Trump real estate investment seminar. Wall Street and it's incestuous 30 year old, Armani dressed, MBA rock star, derivative experts, mortgage backed securities hawkers robbed America's Main Street sending a generation of about to be retirees to jobs at McDonalds and Walmart. Wall Street reamed the U.S. public, walked away without a slap on the wrist and then came back a few years later to buy the distressed properties at discount prices. Talk about a scam.

Making my Mexican real estate business decision even worse, was that at the same time these graying Americans were losing their financial worth they were also being bombarded with daily news reports of how the Mexican drug cartels were killing each other, killing the police, and killing any innocent people who happened to be in their way. Americans no longer had the disposable income to buy second homes in Mexico and also had decided the lure of sitting at the beach drinking a Margarita and becoming part of a shootout just didn't interest them. I was screwed. The only way I could salvage my business was if I could solve two big problems. One, I had to solve the U.S. financial crisis and two, find a new non-violent source of income for the Mexican drug cartels. I had to do it quick. Having only taken Economics 101 and Economics 102 while in college, I couldn't find a solution to fixing the U.S. economy or ending the Mexican Drug war. Boy was I screwed as I watched two years of my life go down the financial toilet.

As I think back on what I thought was the once in a lifetime opportunity for me, I failed to anticipate something that was part of my SWOT Analysis. SWOT is an acronym for Strengths, Weaknesses, Opportunities and Threats. A SWOT analysis is an analysis of a business opportunity where you look at internal strengths and weaknesses that a business owner can control and also at the opportunities and threats that are in the business environment at large and cannot be controlled or influenced by the business.

The first part of my SWOT Analysis - the Strengths and Weaknesses part, included the following strengths: I speak Spanish, I owned a home in Mexico, I had business partners who spoke Spanish, I had a franchising agreement from a major U.S. real estate brokerage to open up in Mexico, I had sold a home in Palo Alto and had some serious cash in hand and I'm also a licensed real estate broker. My weaknesses were that I didn't have a bunch of real estate offices in Mexico and I didn't have any franchising experience. Both these weaknesses could be overcome by bringing in a partner with franchising experience who wanted to help franchisee opens office across Mexico. This was the business opportunity as I saw it.

The second part of my SWOT Analysis - the Opportunity and Threat part, highlighted the BIG OPPORTUNITY as the thousands of Americans, Canadians and Europeans seeking a warm comfortable life abroad. Thousands were already doing it. Why wouldn't more join the party? My party stopper, the thing that killed my business like a squad of cops raiding a high school keg party, were those robbers on Wall Street in their Armani suits and those drug traffickers with AK-47s in Mexico. I simply didn't identify the BIG THREAT of the economy going South and the effect of drug dealers taking over the Board of Tourism in Mexico. It didn't matter that I had my strengths and weaknesses covered in my SWOT analysis, what mattered was that Americans were going broke and had the perception that they would be kidnapped and robbed the second they landed at Cabo San Lucas. The threat part of my SWOT Analysis, the part I couldn't control was just too big an obstacle for me to overcome. My business was screwed and I had to pull the plug after burning through two years of my life without an income and burning through the cash from the sale of a home in Palo Alto. Humbling, to say the least.

Take Away: No matter what business opportunity you're looking at you need to prepare a SWOT Analysis for the business opportunity. Don't underestimate the threats to your business - - the things you can't control. One of the only positive things I got from my Mexican real estate business was the opportunity to travel throughout Mexico and this story I just shared with you. It was the most expensive two years of business school the School of Hard Knocks offered me.

Colonel Sanders Knew His KSF Before Starting KFC

Kentucky Fried Chicken (KFC) serves over 2 BILLION chicken dinners every year and has 11,000 locations in 82 countries around the world. I think every chicken coop in America has on it's wall a picture of every chicken's most hated man - Colonel Harland Sanders. Instead of wearing an orange prison suit, he is wearing his white suit and black string bow tie. Below his picture read the words *"Chicken Murderer: Billions Killed - Run and even Fly if You See Him."* He's recognized by all Americans over age 30 and still scares the hell out of chickens even though he died in 1980 at age 90.

What gave these chickens the heebeegeebees? I think it's the scary story of how Colonel Sanders developed a yummy mixture of 11 herbs and spices and a special pressure cooking process that killed so many of these chicken's forefathers. Scary, but yummy. In 1991 Kentucky Fried Chicken changed its name to KFC as it became one of four or five brands bought under a corporate food chain umbrella. To me, what's amazing about KFC is that Colonel Sanders started franchising his first restaurants at age 65. Who says it's too late for anything, eh? When the Colonel saw that a new highway was being built near his restaurant, and would be diverting traffic around his restaurant's location, he knew the new highway would be the death of his business. He simply wouldn't have the traffic to support his restaurant. Instead of dying and rolling over, he hit the road in his car, traveled the country with his mixture of 11 herbs and spices, and persuaded existing restaurants to join his fold and give him 5 cents for every chicken they sold. In a matter of five years he sold over 600 franchises while his wife stayed home managing the growing business and mixing God knows how many batches of the secret blend used in making KFC chicken.

Colonel Sanders knew two things that every business owner needs to know about if they wish to start a successful business and stay successful in that business. He knew the importance of a SWOT Analysis and KSF. Whenever I meet a wannabe business owner who wants to share their business idea with me, I first always ask to see two things -- their SWOT Analysis and their Key Success Factors Statement (KSF). If you don't know what a SWOT Analysis is, make sure to read *Economics 101* and *AK47's - Your SWOT Analysis* after reading this chapter. Most first drafts of a business' SWOT Analysis and KSF that I see are usually drawn on a napkin and most entrepreneurs I met have never written either document.

We've all heard of the unlucky home owner who rushs into their burning home with only one minute to grab their most prized possessions before their house is reduced to a pile of blackened ash. They need to prioritize what is truly important and be able to do it quickly. Just the same, you should be able to prepare the first draft of your business' KSF like the unlucky home owner with the burning home - Fast. Ask yourself, what are the critical factors you need to address to get your business off the ground? Don't think, grab a napkin and write. What are the first things that come to mind? and you only have one minute to prepare your KSF.

I think Colonel Sanders' KSF probably included the following: a high visibility location with x amount of chicken eaters frequenting each restaurant per day, an economical supply of chicken for each restaurant, chicken that can be cooked quickly, a chicken cooking process that can be duplicated everywhere, a manufacturing and distribution system for those 11 herbs and spices, a unique branded image for KFC, people who believed in his vision and who are willing to be coached in the KFC way, money to live on while driving around selling the franchises, a supportive spouse to co-launch the business, and the willingness to work his ass off while getting things going. Another interesting fact: While starting KFC, Colonel Sanders was already retired and was collecting a monthly social security check of $105 each month.

Take Away: Before you go flush your family finances down the toilet by pulling the trigger on your new business idea, get some napkins and sketch out a SWOT Analysis and KSF. The KSF is the minimum short list of things of must-haves to get your business going. Overlooking or not accurately pre-defining your Key Success Factors will most likely doom your business to the scrap heap of lost American business dreams. If you can't find any napkins to jot down your KSF, head down to your local KFC - I'm sure they've got plenty!

Why Pay Office Rent? 10 Reasons Why Starbucks Can Be Your Startup's Office

It's 6:00 AM on a Friday Morning and I'm sitting at "my office" at the Starbucks café located at the corner of Colorado Avenue and Middlefield Road in Palo Alto, CA. My staff, Louie and Franco the Baristas, Stephen the Display Case King, Jessica and Lulu "The Ambassadors of First Impressions and Happiness", Ariel aka "DJ Solid" and Martha and Art the "The Store Quarterbacks", have my Grande Earl Grey tea ready and my desk is cleaned off and ready for my day. As I sit down I'm greeted by the usual cast of characters; Peter the Austrian business man who speaks *Spanglish*, Kent the political analyst who is funnier than John Stewart and Stephen Colbert, Carolyn the social advocate who Mother Teresa would be proud of, Mark the publisher of a local online newspaper who is out to expose anything and everything wrong about the Palo Alto city government in his own unique way and Boston Bob who sometimes dresses up like George Washington.

<u>10 Reasons Why Starbucks Can Be Your Startup's Office</u>

1. There are over 17,000 Starbucks locations throughout the world. Starbucks is in 50 countries with over 11,000 locations in the United States and at least six locations just in Palo Alto. I think somewhere there must be a Starbucks inside another Starbucks. Where can you get an international network of offices throughout the world and at almost every airport in the

world for free? I think President Obama and all the start-ups owe Starbuck's CEO Howard Schultz a big thank you for providing the millions of start-up owners with a key boot strapping item - free office space.

2. It doesn't cost me one penny to build my office. No lease to sign, no building permits, I don't have to worry about the roof leaking, I don't have to touch up the paint on the walls when a flying skinny caramel machiato is dropped, and I never have to mop the floor.

3. I drink Earl Grey tea. The cost of an Earl Grey tea is under $2.00. Multiple $2.00 x 30 days per month and my monthly rent expense is $60/month and I get 30 cups of tea with free refills to boot.

4. If it's cold outside the heat is on inside Starbucks, if it's hot outside the air-conditioning is turned on inside Starbucks, and if it happens to be nice outside I can sit outside under an umbrella and pet Roxy, my neighbor's dog. Point is, I don't have to pay a utility bill.

5. I don't have to pay a staff to keep the place clean and I've never been to a Starbucks that doesn't have a clean well maintained bathroom. No cleaning fees and I don't have to take out the trash!

6. Free Wi-Fi and lots of plugs to plug in my laptop. Somehow the twisted idea that I have 17,000 routers around the world making me globally connected makes me feel like a Dork Captain of Industry.

7. At my Starbucks business headquarters they offer a wide selection of pastries and sandwiches including a reduced-fat turkey, range free egg white sandwich with the calories even

labeled on it. I call this glorified egg Mcmuffin a "skinny man" and eat it on a regular basis in an effort to keep the spare tire off my belly. As weird as it sounds having the calories labeled on the different foods does make me more conscious of my eating habits.

8. On my birthday, I get a free drink of my choice. Yeah! More free Earl Grey tea!

9. Everyone has heard of Starbucks. When giving directions the Starbuck's logo is universally recognized and all I have to say is I'll meet you at the Starbucks at the corner of so and so and I'm done.

10. The staff at Starbucks tends to be young and in transition. Through the Starbucks staff, I have found a wealth of talent able to help with my business. In fact, the designer of the Web Lunch Box logo, Sophie was working at Starbucks when I hired her. The Starbucks staff can act as your HR staff when it comes to connecting people in the community.

If you're like me, and you're one of the small business people who is able to work out of a Starbucks, here's my recommended list of things to carry in your computer bag: first, and most important, you should have a computer bag that you can roll on the ground (stops you from getting a sore neck or shoulder), a wall plug adapter that you can plug in a single wall outlet and plug in up to three more devices, a six foot extension cord, a ethernet cable and lastly, a cord and charger for your cell phone.

~~Take Away~~: Yes, I deliberately left the strike outs through Take Away.

Weird Fact about Tim Hmelar and Starbucks:

I don't drink coffee.   Also, if you ever try and get an unscheduled appointment with me -- look out. My 11 year old daughter Gracia, who is my executive assistant, and likes her Daddy/Daughter time, and if you don't have an appointment, may prevent you from squatting at my world headquarters meeting room.

When the Going Gets Tough the Weak Jump Ship - and Leave You to Clean Up the Mess

One of the biggest mistakes I made in business was going into business with a friend who needed money more than he desired to build a business. Before deciding to work with him, my friend had recently experienced some personal issues and was trying to get back on his feet. I thought I could be a good friend and help out. I would help him and thought he could help me grow my business. Everyone would win. Boy, was I wrong!

His now ex-wife no longer talks to me, he quit the business with no notice, never paid back a personal loan that I vouched for him (I ended up paying it back) and had to face another good friend tell me "I hate to say it, but I told you so. I told you to be careful with him and that he had burned one of my friends in a business deal." The whole thing became a big mess and I no longer have anything to do with this person. Here are some rules I think worthy of sharing with you:

1. If you're starting a new business, DON'T go into business with people who need a job; go into business with people who

are passionate about the business and want to be paid for their contribution and are willing to get paid a modest salary to cover their personal expenses while the business is getting its wings. Start-up mode is not the time to get financially fat.

2. Don't allow your business partners to make bank withdrawals or write checks over $500.00 and if the money is really needed, require two signatures for any withdrawals over $500.00. Back to my old friend, he raped the company bank account and then quit leaving the company without notice. I later found out he did the same thing to his ex-wife with a business they had owned. Just as he did with me, he walked out on his wife, and left her holding the bag and mop to clean up the mess.

3. Be very careful of working with people who have recently become sober. They may be off the booze or coke but may have not grown to operate with integrity, and may, if necessary, have not re-calibrated their moral compass. In my case, after paying my soon to be vanishing business partner over $64,000.00, he asked me to, instead of report the money I paid him as income, to report it as a loan so he wouldn't have to pay alimony or child support to his wife who was in the process of divorcing him. I refused to go along with his request and told him it was wrong to be thinking this way. This was the time I knew my business partner had lost his moral compass. I should have seen the writing on the wall that I would be receiving the short end of the stick in the near future - and I did.

4. Do not sign personal guarantees for business partners who are having financial troubles. In my case, I ate close to $6,000 paying back money my business partner borrowed, never re-payed and that I never touched.

5. Road Kill is the Model to Pay Hired Guns. Don't pay someone a lot of money to close deals without them closing deals. If someone tells you *"I'm the best at closing deals and will get the business lots of customers,"* give them a small base salary with huge kickers for closing deals and let them prove to you they really can close deals. The arrangement should describe a time frame for closing the deals, the number of deals, the size of the deals and what the kicker is for successfully completing the deals. No deals, no kickers. No deals after a defined period of time - there's the door, don't let it hit you in the keister on the way out. Oh yeah, and BTW no stock or ownership rights have vested.

6. Check out prospective biz partners references. In my case, I was asked point blank by a very successful friend of mine *"Timmy are you sure about so and so? I've heard some serious bad stuff about him and if I were you I'd be very careful about working with him."* It was very humbling to say the least when I got to hear the big I TOLD YOU SO from my successful friend. Some good questions to ask a prospective business partner are *"Tell me about your biggest business blunder? What have you learned from it? Did anyone got pissed off at your actions and how do you feel about it?"* Check out the references no matter how well you think you know the person. Everyone, including me, has skeletons in the closet.

7. Once you've weathered the ugly business partner storm, it's time to move on. Honestly, I was pissed for two years at my ex-friend, ex-business partner for all the stuff he did. Who wouldn't? What I learned from the experience, though, is that holding on to anger has done nothing to help me move on and focus on my family and business. In my case, I don't think my ex-business partner loses one wink of sleep for his actions. He still sleeps like a baby and dreams about the next business he

can get his fingers in. For my part, I learned I was very naive to trust this person. I screwed up and have learned some expensive lessons I hope you never have to experience I've moved on, am not angry anymore, have no interest in crossing paths with this person and on the bright side he gave me the content for this chapter which hopefully you'll never have to experience firsthand.

Take Away: Be very careful about going into business with friends/business partners who are weathering a personal storm. If they have nothing to lose, their problems may become your problems. Trusting business partners with keys to the piggy bank can cost you lots of money and tarnish your reputation. Remember when the going gets tough, the weak abandon ship and they are the first ones on the lifeboat in search of another ship to latch on to.

Networking

Gate Keepers Suck: How to Literally Get Your Foot in the Door and Talk with Anyone

In the early 1980s while attending San Jose State University, I developed the habit of reading all the major business magazines and newspapers (Google, websites and blogs didn't exist back then). Whenever I read an article that made a special impression on me, I would write the author and share with them my thoughts about their article and ask if I could meet them. One such author I contacted was Jack Falvey who had written an article in the Wall Street Journal about physical contact between people in the workplace. It was the weirdest article I had ever read in the WSJ. However, Jack is the greatest sales expert I've ever been blessed to cross paths with and he's the one who taught me how to get your foot in the door and talk with anyone. To this day Jack and I remain friends and I visit him whenever I can when I'm in Boston. If you'd like to learn more about Jack Falvey check him out at www.falvey.org.

<u>True Story: The one shoe in the door trick.</u>

I wanted to talk with the founders of Home Depot. Arthur Blank and Bernie Marcus are the founders of Home Depot and they have written a book called <u>Built From Scratch</u> which tells the story of Home Depot's beginning. I read the book and noticed in a picture that Bernie Marcus is rather tall and Arthur Blank appeared to be rather short. I went to Target and bought two pairs of work boots; one pair size 12 and the other size 9.

Overnight, I FedEx's Bernie one of the size 12 boots and Arthur one of the size 9 boots. Accompanying each boot was a short note that said *"I've got one foot in the door and I need to get the other foot in the door. I'll call you tomorrow at 10 AM."* The next day I called Home Depot's main switch board and asked to speak with Bernie Marcus and was put through to his secretary. Bernie's secretary, a friendly woman, asked me how she could help me. When I told her I had sent Bernie an overnight package and I believed he was expecting my call, she responded by saying, *"Are you the boot man?"* I responded *"yes"* and she said we've all been expecting your call and 10 seconds later I was speaking with Bernie.

Take Away: Don't be afraid to be *"Younique"* and think outside of the box. Busy executives are inundated with meeting requests and have coached their staff to screen calls and keep a wall between them and the annoying interruptions they encounter every day. If you want to meet or talk to someone you must stand out of the crowd to get their attention. Using creative introduction tactics I have been able to get in front of Bob Noyce the founder of Intel and inventor of the integrated circuit, , Bob Tillman the CEO of Lowe's, Pitch Johnson the Grand Daddy of venture capital at Asset Management Company and many other influential business leaders.

Mommy Told Me NOT to Talk to Strangers - Mommy Lied

True Story. I have a friend who many years ago walked into a restaurant and took a seat in the waiting area while waiting to be seated. As he was waiting for his table, he struck up a conversation with a young man who said he was the founder of a computer company. As the two talked and shared their business experiences, they introduced themselves to one another; the older man saying *"My name is Jay Elliot,"* and the younger man saying *"My name is Steve Jobs. It's nice to meet you."* Elliot, who had just left Intel, found himself in a new job. He became Steve Job's ~~Right~~ Left Hand Man. FYI, Steve Jobs was left-handed and Jay Elliot was hired by Jobs to be Apple's Senior Vice President. Later Elliot went on to write *The Steve Jobs Way - iLeadership for a New Generation,* a book that tells the story of the two working together. If Jobs and Elliot had followed their mother's advice to not talk to strangers, they never would have met.

While studying business at San Jose State University in the early 1980's, I was fortunate to have Wanda Blockhus as my *Intro to Marketing* Professor. Professor Blockhus took a special interest in me - both in and out of the classroom. She suggested I join AIESEC, an international work exchange program for college students, and also suggested I write to one successful and influential business person per week. Take note, those were the pre-internet days. So, I had subscriptions to the Wall Street Journal, Asian Wall Street Journal, The San Jose Business Journal, Business Week, Venture Magazine and some other magazines that I can't even remember the names. Anyway, I would read these different newspapers and magazines and would pick one lucky writer per week to write to tell them what I thought about their article and ask to meet with them. The response to my letters at first was slow, but soon I was being invited to Boston, New York City, Los Angeles, San Francisco and Washington D.C. to meet people. Every person I wrote to was blown away by my initiative and was happy to meet with me. Thank God Wanda Blockhus knew the power of meeting strangers and passed that knowledge on to me. Today, I still remain friends with some of these business people who I met more than 30 years ago.

With the advent of social media, it's easier to meet people than ever. You don't have to leave your house or office to meet some of the world's most interesting people -- people who generally are more than happy to help you out provided you have good netiquette. I wrote a chapter about *Etiquette, Netiquette and How To Hold a Fork*, you should check that out after this.

LinkedIn is my favorite place for meeting strangers online. LinkedIn has a feature called Groups where people can join or start groups that attract people with common interests or businesses. As I'm writing this I just went to LinkedIn, logged in and went and looked at the groups I'm a member of. One of the LinkedIn groups I'm a member of is called *Marketing to Over 50's: Old People, Grey's, Retirees, Seniors & Pensioners*. I clicked on the group and found an article called *7 Ways to Develop Your Key Words & Feed the Search Spiders* written by Patty Cisco - Principal & Creative Catalyst. I've never met Patty in person before and I don't even know where she's at right now. However, I do know that not only do Patty and I have a common interest in Marketing to Over 50's, but we are also interested in

SEO and ways of optimizing traffic to websites. Patty is a stranger I'm interested in meeting and I am going to introduce myself. Thank you, LinkedIn, for converting a total stranger into a new biz associate.

Millions of people swear by Yelp and its reviews. Yelp is the world's largest reviewing social networking website that allows Joe Blow the Consumer to write reviews online detailing his experiences with different businesses. Yelp is the biggest freak show of strangers I've ever been involved with. I personally don't know many of the 78 million plus people who write reviews on Yelp but I do tend to trust these strangers more than any advertising piece written by any company's advertising department. Why? Most strangers don't have anything to lose or gain by critiquing a business. I look at the different reviews written by my stranger friends, weed out the psycho reviews and the reviews obviously written by the business owner, and come up with my own opinion on whether to frequent a business establishment or service based on the collective opinions of my stranger Yelp buddies. In the end, I tend to trust most of my Yelper buddies even though they're strangers. I suggest you read (and take by heart) the chapter that I wrote about how you must *Do Your Barbequing in the Backyard - Don't Let Your Business get Barbequed on YELP.*

Take Away: Mom was wrong. Talking to strangers is a good thing. Don't be afraid to smile and meet new people and don't be afraid to invite some really cool strangers over to your house or business by logging on to LinkedIn or Yelp.

Postscript: My mother recently told me it's okay to talk to strangers as long as you don't do it while using Skype and in the bathroom. Okay Mom, you're right about this one.

Etiquette, Netiquette and How to Hold a Fork

We've all known people who lack social skills, you know; the people who never hold the door open for someone, who leave a room without saying goodbye, who chew gum while public speaking and who hold a fork like a caveman eating a woolly mastodon. Whether you like it or not, people pick up on your etiquette, netiquette and how you hold a fork.

Netiquette is nothing more than etiquette for our online communications. Use netiquette properly and people will love you; use it wrong and you will piss someone off. Recently, I had a Facebook friend pay someone to set up his social media accounts which included auto-posting and syndicating his Foursquare account to his Facebook Business Page. This person not only likes to frequent many different places he likes to tell everyone where he is and soon started posting to Foursquare every place he was at. I kid you not, I received at least 10 different posts per day to my Facebook wall announcing where this friend was eating, buying gas, working out at the gym, shopping for toothpaste and on and on. I think the only thing he didn't post was when he was in the bathroom. Anyways, his posts were just a bunch of spam to me. I sent him a private message asking him to stop and he responded he didn't know how to stop the syndicating. After one more day of his nonsense, I hid ALL HIS POSTS from my Facebook wall and I haven't had to deal with his updates since then. Furthermore, I will never recommend a client of mine to work with this person because I fear he will start posting all his garbage to my friends Facebook pages.

Another no-no is using a Facebook personal page for your business. To use your personal Facebook page to promote your business is against the Facebook terms and conditions and I've known two different people who have been kicked off Facebook for trying to sell real estate on their personal Facebook Pages. In order to create a Facebook Business page you must have a Facebook personal page. If you're one of those people who doesn't want to create a Facebook Personal page because you don't want people interfering with your personal life you should know you can create a Facebook personal page that basically has all the content hidden from the public.

Never forget Social Media is called Social Media for a reason. It's supposed to be SOCIAL. The way I was raised social means to interact with others in a mutually beneficial way. It doesn't mean dominating a conversation, never listening and ignoring others. It's not about YOU, it's about OTHERS and creating relationships where everyone wins. I know of a woman who promotes herself as a content writing coach who likes to blast me with e-mails promoting her business and why I should take her classes and give her money. On two different occasions, I have sent her e-mails asking questions about her services and she has never replied. All I've ever received from her are her e-mails telling me how wonderful she is and that I should give her money. It's weird to me that she bills herself as the content writing Goddess, but lacks netiquette.

Case in point. While I was attending San Jose State University in the early 1980's I was asked to be the keynote speaker to a group of about 100 businesswomen and businessmen in Los Gatos, CA. The talk was about the benefits of using international students from an organization called AIESEC to help grow these businessmen and businesswomen's businesses. My talk was only about 20 minutes long and I shared how APPLE, IBM, HP and others were using the program. After I finished speaking, and after dinner, I was approached by a Vice President of a major New York City publishing company and asked to fly to New York to see if I wanted to work with him. I asked *"Why would you want me to come work for you?"* and his reply was *"I know you can speak in front of large audiences and I saw how you hold a fork and I know you would never embarrass our organization."*

Take Away: Know Your Netiquette and if you're a cavemen or cavewomen when it comes to holding a fork and you ever have to sit down face to face at a client meal, learn how to hold a fork today.

It's Not Connecting the Dots. You Need to Stumble Upon Dots You Didn't Know Exist

We've all heard the old adage about "connecting the dots." In my life, the most valuable dots I've ever connected with were dots not found on my radar screen. Whether you're in the Dry Cleaning Business or creating the newest cutting edge technology, having the ability to find dots (opportunities) off your business radar screen can make the difference between your business failing, moderately succeeding or kicking butt and taking names. The key to finding dots that aren't on your radar screen is to intentionally put yourself in places and with people who aren't familiar and who you probably won't find comfortable on the first encounter.

"It's not a matter of getting out of your "comfort zone" – most people are not living a comfortable or fulfilling life. Instead, it's a matter of MAKING THE DECISION to get out of your "familiar zone" by overcoming your fears and lack of enthusiasm for life; and then writing and implementing your own life plan". - *Tim Hmelar*

Three Keys to Finding Dots Off Your Radar Screen:

1. If you must eat lunch with the same people every day, then at least have breakfast with someone new once a week. Make it a point to meet new people every day,

listen to them and then in your own little ways help them achieve their goals. This may require you to shut up and listen for a change. If and when you talk, you should ask questions to learn more about the speaker's needs and then see if you can contribute either a piece of information to the speaker or make an introduction for them to someone who can help. As the speaker shares information with you, it is vital you keep your networking antenna up to see if the speaker is sharing off the radar screen dots (introductions or information) that could be valuable to you. Remember, first thing is to help others achieve their goals.

Ken Yap, a friend of mine that I met on Facebook, is a master of helping others become successful while planting seeds of relationships that help him grow his financial planning business. After bumping into each other on Facebook, Ken and I literally met for the first time for breakfast at a bakery in Cupertino, California. The one thing I know about Ken (better known as the "Yapster") is that he authentically loves helping others be more successful. If you wish to connect with Ken, check Ken out on Facebook at Facebook.com/KenYap – I bet you Ken will introduce you to a dot that will be valuable to your business.

If you've got big balls, make eye contact with people you don't know and introduce yourself. If things go well, and if possible, try and sit down with the person for a quick chat to find out what they're all about with the goal of helping them. If you're really into expanding your network and are open to meeting strangers, read Timothy Ferriss' *The Four Hour Work Week*. In his book, Tim describes an exercise on how to make new contacts without getting beaten up or arrested for stalking. FYI, I use this tactic every week and it drives my kids crazy - for the life of them, my kids Fe, Seattle and Gracia can't believe I deliberately go out of my way to talk with strangers at coffee shops, farmers markets, bookstores or the beach.

2. It's not just about belly button to belly button networking anymore. With sites such as Facebook, Twitter and LinkedIn, mouse to mouse is the equivalent of attending a mixer computer to computer.   The cool thing about networking online is you don't have to get in your car and travel, you don't have to dress up and you don't have to pay any fees. If you're wondering, yes, I use old school places to meet people like Chamber of Commerce business mixers, BNI networking meetings, and trade association meetings but I also use LinkedIn Groups, Twitter Searches, Facebook Groups and make comments on blogs in an effort to find dots not on my radar screen. I have met clients by attending trade meetings such as SILVAR for the real estate industry, NARI for the construction industry, and Home Town Peninsula (a Menlo Park, CA trade organization for locally owned business owners.)   More and more, the old school belly button to belly button groups are bolstering their online presence in addition to promoting social gatherings where people actually meet in person.

3. Another great place I have found for meeting "influential movers and shakers who are also givers" is at places where people either exercise or worship. I don't have scientific results but almost all of the super successful people I know take their health seriously and take their spirituality seriously. FYI, the root of the word health means "to make whole" and the root of the word spirituality means "to breathe" as in to breathe life into yourself and others.

I like to run around The Dish, a trail on Stanford University's campus. When running The Dish, I make it a point to say hello to every person that I encounter on my run. As a matter of fact, on Friday mornings I wear a shirt that my kids made for me that says *"High Five Friday"* on the front and *"Have a Nice Day"* on the back. On Fridays, I greet everyone I see by giving them a High Five while I yell out *"Its High Five Friday."* After two years of High Five Fridays, I literally have hundreds of people who greet me with a High Five whenever they see me. I have had people approach me in restaurants, at a funeral, even in traffic where they ask me, *"Hey aren't you Mr. High Five Friday."* God forbid if I miss my Friday run, because the next week I'm grilled about where I was the past week.

So what's the big deal about High Five Friday? It has opened doors to relationships I couldn't have imagined. While running The Dish, I met Efi Luzon, one of the nation's top commercial real estate agents. In time, Efi and I have developed a strong friendship and business relationship that had its beginnings based on our love of running. The other cool thing about meeting Efi was getting his perspective of the world and business based on his strong Jewish faith and his life experiences. I have learned more about Judaism and commercial real estate from my running chats with Efi more than with anyone else.

Take Away: Deliberately put yourself in new environments with new people to be able to find dots that can catapult your business to the next level.

Ducks Don't Soar With Eagles and Ostriches and Humming Birds Don't Fly South Together

Your life will mirror the lives of the five people you spend the most time with. Birds of the same feather do flock together. Ducks don't soar with eagles and ostriches and humming birds don't fly South together. Successful business people socialize and network with other successful people. Successful people don't hang out with losers. People who don't exercise, lounge with others who don't exercise as well. People who value their health don't eat junk food, don't smoke, don't do drugs or don't buy a six pack of beer every night to drink while watching Jersey Shore or Basket Ball Wives. Poor people hang out with other poor people. Rich people don't hang out with poor people. Rich people do things differently than poor people and that's how they became rich. People who make $25,000/year hang out with others who make $25,000/year and people who make $250,000/year tend to hang out with other people who make $250,000/year. I could go on all day with more examples of birds of a feather flocking together but you'd get bored and stop reading this chapter. That's simply the way it is.

So if you're just finishing school or you're already in business and you want to network up with other successful entrepreneurs and business people, how do you get things kick started? How do you join the club you aspire to join? Quite simply, you must market yourself to gain access to these people. You must market yourself to gain acceptance and build trust with these people, and you must communicate with these people to build confidence and take the time to foster the relationship. Do this and you'll be able to enter new groups that can change your life. In my experience, most successful people can remember a time when they were trying to move up the business ladder and most are open to helping aspiring business people who appear to be sincere and motivated to make changes in their life.

In the early 1980's, I was an undergrad studying business at San Jose State University and I was also helping a Professor with a book he was writing on technology and Japanese business practices. As part of our work, I suggested we interview Bob Noyce who is one of the founders of Intel and inventor of the integrated circuit. My professor thought it was a great idea but that the odds of Bob Noyce taking time out of his schedule to meet with me were next to zero. Anyway, being the stubborn idealist I am, I ignored my professor, called the switchboard at Intel and asked to speak to Bob Noyce. Within 30 seconds I was talking with Bob and within two minutes he invited me to come and meet with him. When I met him a couple of days later, I asked him why he took the time to meet with me. He answered that he remembered when he was starting out that many people helped him, that his parents had raised him to help others, and that I seemed like a nice guy on the phone. After my meeting with Bob he opened up his rolodex to me and made many phone call introductions on my behalf to many of Silicon Valley's leading entrepreneurs and venture capitalists.

If you don't believe me about birds of a feather flocking together, I suggest you do the following exercise. Write down the five names of the people you spend the most time with. If you have a spouse and kids mark down one of the five people as a collective "spouse and kids."

Maybe your list is something like this: spouse and kids, my office worker Joe, my best friend Tom, my running partner Efi, and my brother Frank. Now write down what you think is the yearly salary for each of these five people and describe their physical health by rating them on a scale from 1-5 with one being poor health and 5 being excellent heatlh. Add the numbers together for their yearly salary and again for their physical health and divide it by five. In most cases when I've coached people on this process they find out the result is very close to their yearly income and the status of their health. In most cases they weren't happy with the answer.

Take Away: If you want to change your life, change your income, your business, your relationships, your spirituality or your physical wellbeing I have found that most people need to change some of the five people they spend most of their time with. Honestly ask a successful biz person for a 30 minute coffee meeting, go running with someone successful, join a entrepreneurs/small biz owners group and introduce yourself, read blogs or newspapers and contact the authors. The key is to intentionally target new people to spend time with.

Legal

You May Not be Bi, But Some of Your Contracts Are - Bilateral and Unilateral Contracts

When I was in college, I took two different law classes - Intro to Business Law and Business Ethics.   I learned that for me business law is boring, hard to understand and that I needed to learn a whole bunch of new words and new meanings for words I thought I already knew. Before taking Intro to Business Law, I thought the word 'consideration' meant being sensitive to the needs or feelings of others. But in business law, it was totally different. I learned that 'consideration' is something of value being given by one party to a contract to the other party who is then obligated to do or not do something. In Business Ethics I learned how to write legal briefs and learned that many businesses, in the pursuit of making money, are not ethical at all. Finally I learned that almost any lawyer can take two radically opposing views on an issue depending on your directions as a client and if you have the money to pay them. No wonder I never went to law school.

I live in Palo Alto, California, and depending on who you talk to, Palo Alto is supposedly the birthplace of Silicon Valley.   If Palo Alto is truly the birth place of Silicon Valley, I think every other city on the San Francisco Peninsula is confused about where Silicon Valley really started.   How can Palo Alto, San Jose,

Mountain View, Santa Clara or Sunnyvale all be the birthplace of Silicon Valley? And quite frankly, who gives a hoot?

I prefer to say I live in what used to be called Silicon Valley and is now called Social Media Alley. In my mind, Social Media Alley runs from Mountain View to San Francisco. It's as if Social Media Valley swallowed Silicon Valley. Social Media Alley is still home to Apple, Intel, HP and Cisco but I see more press for Google, Facebook, Twitter, Yelp, LinkedIn, WordPress, Instagram, Pinterest and YouTube than I do for Silicon Valley semiconductor companies. San Francisco, besides being home to Yelp, Twitter and WordPress in case you haven't heard, is ground zero for Humanity's Love Fest where every kind of life style is not only embraced but is celebrated.

Every conceivable lifestyle and cause is celebrated in San Francisco. Chinese New Year, Cinco de Mayo, The Hookers Ball, 49ers and Giants Fans. Want to run a race naked? Try the Bay to Breakers. Like swimming? How about the Alcatraz Sharkfest Swim? Feel like expressing your inner hippy? Visit Haight Ashbury, Want to express your sexuality? Try San Francisco's Pride the city's celebration for Lesbian, Gay, Bisexual, and Transgender San Franciscans.

As a business owner it doesn't matter whether you're a breeder, gay, straight or bi; you need to know the difference between bilateral and unilateral contracts. Most people won't ask you about your sexual orientation on a daily basis; however, many people will ask you to enter into a contract with them on a daily basis. Some contracts will be verbal and some contracts written, some will be bilateral and some will be unilateral. Sometimes, you won't even notice that you have engaged in a contract at all!

A bilateral contract is a contract where the two parties to the contract agree to perform pre-defined acts. Each party agrees to do or not do something in exchange for the other party agreeing to do or not do something. Simply put, Party A agrees to do something in exchange for Party B agreeing to do something. Example of a Bilateral Contract with my company Web Lunch Box. Want to attend a conference on how small businesses can use social media? Web Lunch Box agrees to host a hands-on social media conference where you can participate in classes taught by employees of Google, Facebook, LinkedIn and other companies for an attendance fee of $99. Party A - Web Lunch Box promises to host a series of classes for you to participate in, if you, Party B promise to pay Web Lunch Box $99. Both parties agree to do something and are obligated to act on their promise. Get it? It's pretty basic and we see these contracts happen every day.

Other examples of bilateral contracts are:

1. A business owner agreeing to pay a cleaning business $200/month to clean their office every two weeks
2. A person agreeing to pay a web designer $2,000 to build a website
3. An attorney agreeing to write a collection letter (better known as a Nasty Gram) to a non-paying customer for $500
4. Southwest Airlines agreeing to fly you to your business meeting in NYC for $500,
5. A pharmaceutical company agreeing to pay you money for you agreeing to drop a lawsuit and for you agreeing to NOT disclose the terms of the agreement, or
6. Daffy Dave, a clown friend of mine, agreeing to entertain your 7 year olds birthday guests for $300.

You get the picture. The list goes on and on.

A unilateral contract is very different than a bilateral contract. With a unilateral contract, a business/person makes a promise to do something for another business/person who is not obligated to act, if the business/person who is not obligate to act, does act, the business/person making the initial promise is obligated to fulfill the original promise.

Too much to understand? Let this example help you. Unilateral Contract Example: You're at a baseball game watching the Oakland A's play the Boston Red Sox. Your three kids Fe, Seattle, and Gracia (the names of my three kids) jump up screaming "Daddy, we want Dippin Dots Icecream!" You look over and see an exhausted, sun parched dude laboring up the stairways carrying Dippin Dots. He's yelling out "Dippin Dots - Gettin Yaaaaaaaah Dippin Dots - Dippin Dots - 5 Dollars!" The ice cream vendor is actually initiating a unilateral contract. None of the fans are obliged to buy the Dippin Dots; however, as soon as someone passes five bucks across the row of seats to the ice cream vendor, the ice cream vendor is obligated to perform: to toss a container of Dippin Dots at my kids. The unilateral contract has been consummated and my kids are happy.

Most contracts between business owners and consumers at restaurants, bars and retail establishments are unilateral. These types of transactions are also called B to C transactions (business to consumer). Most contracts between businesses involve bilateral contracts and are called B to B transactions (business to business).

As easy as the examples above may be, sometimes it can be confusing to determine if a contract is bilateral or unilateral. In disputes, our almighty justice system (that pampers to the rich and Hollywood) tends

to try and determine if both parties made promises to the contract, provided consideration, and if so, when. Doesn't that last sentence I wrote suck and sound confusing? I told you I didn't like business law and, all the confusing words and their convoluted interpretations and meanings.

Take Away: People come in all kinds of sexual preferences and contracts do too. Unilateral, Gay, Straight, Bilateral or Bisexual -- the world of law and citizens of San Francisco come in all shapes and sizes. Know your business contracts and find the time to visit Silicon Valley, Social Media Alley, or San Francisco and let your *"Younique"* legal freak flag fly.

If You're Not Dicking Around With Your Business, Use a Non-Disclosure Agreement

Something I've learned in business is that most people are actually good people with a great deal of integrity. They want you to be successful, and most will really go out of their way to help you along on your own way. These are the people you can trust. They're the type of person that if you dropped your wallet in the street or if you left your cell phone on a restaurant table, they would pick it up and chase you down the street to give it to you.

I've also learned that there are some real bad people who will smile at you while they intentionally scheme on how to take advantage of you. These people are like sugar coated piranha fish and spotting them in the busy business world is next to impossible. They will eat you alive by stealing your idea, filing frivolous lawsuits, stealing money from the company bank account and finding dumbass reasons not to pay their bills. These are the same people who park their car in handicap parking spots even when they're not handicapped. Many are sociopaths that have no sense of empathy on how their actions affect others. I personally believe these people are mentally ill and lack the gene that gives a person a moral compass. If you believe in *karma,* these are the people who will be reborn as cockroaches, only to be crushed in their next life.

If you'll ask me how to stay clear of the psychos in your community, I don't have an answer for you on that. As a matter of fact, it's impossible NOT to run into these people unless you lock yourself in your house and never go outside. Even then it's just a matter of time before you run into one online.   If these life sucking users only make up 1% of your community, you probably will bump into at least 2-10/day. Most will not harm you in any way unless you decide to have a relationship with them. Remember getting that funny feeling about a person at times? Well then, that's the Almighty Business God telling you to run away as fast as you can.   Follow the hunch in your stomach if you get one.

If you're Not Dicking Around with your business, a Non-Disclosure Agreement (NDA) is a form you should be familiar with. It's the business equivalent of a pinky promise between two 13 year olds swearing not to share secrets revealed at an overnight sleepover.   Same commitment, only legally documented. In short, it's an agreement where two parties swear not to reveal or share sensitive information outside the relationship. If the information is shared, one of the parties to the agreement could be harmed and therefore in the interest of both parties, he wants to make sure confidential information is not leaked.

Examples of information protected under an NDA may include that a business owner asks a real estate broker not to disclose who the buyer of a certain property is, that Facebook is looking to sign a lease in Menlo Park, that a software developer is not to share information about a new program being developed, or that an out of court settlement has been reached and that terms agreed upon are not to be divulged. Simply put, NDA's are "zippers" on the mouths of businesses and people.

If you must share invaluable information with someone, have them sign a NDA. It doesn't matter whether this person is your best friend from college, a previous business partner, or the Dalai Lama. Have them sign it or keep your lips zipped. Remember you're Not Dicking Around with your financial future and remember there are people who will deliberately lie through their teeth in order to take advantage of you. This is one time I believe being paranoid is healthy.

Venture Capitalists won't sign NDAs. I've been blessed to meet many venture capitalists throughout the years. The first real VC I got to meet was "Pitch" Johnson, the Grand Daddy of Silicon Valley VC. I was a long-haired 22 year old business student at SJSU when Bob Noyce (founder of Intel) called Pitch and asked him to meet with me. It was a day I will always remember. But here's one thing I've learned about VC's and executives of large companies. They won't sign NDA's. Yep, you read it right - they won't sign your NDA. Why not, you ask? Venture Capitalists see tons of deals all day long and for them to sign a document about something you're about to share could be business suicide. If they were to sign your NDA, they may have already seen your idea somewhere else and now they'd be bound not to share it or capitalize on it. It's bad business for them, therefore, good luck trying to get them to sign one. If you're seeking funding from a VC, you must put together a killer *preso* and have faith you're not talking to some unscrupulous vulture capitalist.

Take Away: Successful business people are paranoid when it comes to sharing proprietary information. They let others know they are Not Dicking Around. Most importantly, they know when and where to use an NDA. Sure, life and business is all about taking risks. But being paranoid can be healthy and can even make you rich.

It Takes a Thief/My $52,000 Lawyer Bill: Read this if You're Hiring a Programmer or Sub-Contractor

One thing I don't understand about law in the United States is how the Courts have set the precedent that software belongs to the person who writes it even if the person writing the software has been hired and paid as a subcontractor to write the software for someone else.   Okay, let's run through that again. I pay someone to write software for my company but I don't own the right to do whatever I want with the software and the person who wrote the software actually owns it? Yep, that's right. WTF!

Some years ago, I designed all the screenshots for a piece of software and wrote all the algorithms for the program to run. I then gave my work to a programmer who wrote some code for my company.   After the software was developed, my programmer told me he owned the software and that I wasn't able to let other people use the software because he owned it and he now wanted to own 51% of my company (his 51% ownership would have let him call all the shots with the business I had started) because he wrote the software for me. When I talked to an intellectual property attorney, he told me unless I had a contract assigning all the rights to me, the programmer was right and that I should negotiate with the programmer. To say I was pissed off is an understatement. I spent the better part of a year talking to the programmer through an attorney where I spent $52,000 on attorney fees trying to get the programmer to acquiesce on his demand for 51% ownership of my company. Finally without having a resolution with the programmer, I had my attorney tell the programmer's attorney that the programmer could go to hell and I moved forward with a new programmer who signed a document assigning all the work he was being hired to do for my company to my company.

Take Away: Unless you have $52,000.00 to flush down the toilet and if you're developing software, make sure your contract with the developer assigns all the rights of the software and any derivative work (additional work based on the original work) to you or your business. Also if you're having any artwork, logos, trademarks, websites, blogs or anything developed by another person make sure all the rights to the work have been assigned to you before getting started with any outside consultant.

Time Management

Daddy, Can We Spend Some Shi*ty Time Together? Why Quality Time Doesn't Exist

In my many years living and working in Silicon Valley (I mean Social Media Alley), I can't count how many times I've heard fathers tell me *"I don't spend a lot of time with my family, but when I do it's quality time."* I got so tired of hearing this bull that when I hear it now I look them squarely in the face and tell them they're full of crap.

Fact is, either you're a quality person or you're not. You can't be a quality person some of the time and a slacker the rest of the time.

Simply put QUALITY TIME DOESN'T EXIST

I'd love to see the following scenario play out.

> Ring, ring, ring. *"Hey Johnny, this is Daddy. I'm so sorry you haven't seen me much the last 2-3 years but how about we meet and spend some quality time together? I promise we'll do whatever you want for 10-15 minutes with no interruptions. What do you think? You game?"*

Then Johnny says, *"Hey Dad, thanks for the offer but I'm really tired and really don't know who you are. How about we get together for those 10-15 minutes and spend some crappy time together? I'm not up for quality time but some crappy time sounds good. I'd love to share with you how you missed my first Little League game, how you're always distracted with cell phone calls and texts, and how you missed me getting the "Student of the Week" award at school. Let's not forget when you forgot my birthday, and I'd also like to introduce you to Mr. Smith, my football coach who someone recently mistook as you. Oh yeah, while we're at it maybe we should talk about how Mom thinks you're an ass and that you're not the man she married. I can't tell you how much I'm looking forward to our crappy time together and telling one another how much we kind of love each other."*

When overbooked parents or partners don't spend time with their children or spouses, it's no surprise to see the neglected children or neglected spouse having emotional problems. The most common feeling is the feel of being unloved and unwanted and the most common effect is falling in to depression; gravitating to drugs, alcohol and other vices or affairs. Like I said, quality time doesn't exist and if you're not living your life as a quality person, you should schedule some of your so called quality time to put out fires with the school counselor, family therapist, divorce attorney or bartender.

If you think quality time exists, you're wrong. Before you start your grandiose spiel about how your start-up or long work hours are for the good of your family, you might want to check with them to see if they agree with you. By spending time with your loved ones, they realize the extent of your love for them. By being engaged and focused when you are with them, they know that they are far more important than anything else in this world. This is how you show your love to them – by spending time with them and meeting their emotional needs rather than just fulfilling their financial needs.

Your kids really don't care about how hard you work today supposedly in their long term interest. What they really want is for you to attend their sports events, to put the phone down when you're with them, be at some of their school functions, be at their birthday, coach their team or spend some time advising their special interest and if you're married creating a happy home with your spouse.

Take Away: So what are you – a quality person or an over-booked person serving bull?

Let's Do the Time Warp Again: You No Longer Have Set Work Hours - Mesh Time

Do you wear a watch? I don't. Most of my friends don't wear watches either. One thing I do though is take my iPhone with me everywhere I go. Customers and businesses have evolved to the *"No, I can't wait generation."* The idea of set business hours has gone out the window. From 8-5, to flex time, the world now does business on what I call "Mesh Time."

Business communication is now expected to be "meshed" in everywhere you go and at any time. People "gobble" information in small bites throughout the day anywhere they happen to be. People talk and text in their cars while stopped at traffic lights or in line at the bank. People now store their documents on the cloud; and easily and quickly send business orders while sitting at the local coffee shop or the beach. I don't know how many business conversations I've had while exercising and running at The Dish on Stanford's campus. People update their Facebook business profile while in line ordering tacos. The line between personal time and business time doesn't exist for most people. You have one life -- and your business and personal time have become meshed together. We've all become technological turkeys who gobble information throughout the day.

Here's the interesting thing I've found out about being available 24/7 anytime anywhere. For most communications, it doesn't matter if you're always available. Be truthful -- how many times have you received a life or death phone call? Something so important that if you didn't answer immediately something horrible would happen to you or your loved ones? I can count on one hand how many times I've had to answer a text, e-mail or phone call immediately.

Knowing that most things can wait is good to know. Knowing that people are "gobbling" information is also good to know even if you don't respond immediately. Most "gobbling" of information is done on cell phones or mobile devices. In an effort to serve your customer base, it is important to make sure you have a strong web presence that is designed to be viewed on mobile devices.

If you're a business person, being available 24/7 is a double edge sword. At times it's great to be available anywhere any time; other times it just doesn't make sense or the urgency doesn't exist to communicate whenever your customers contact you. If you're spending time with your family, I'm sure your kids and spouse don't want you to be constantly interrupted by phone calls and texts. Ironically, in my state California, it's illegal to text while driving even though I see it every day.

Some suggestions to keep your sanity and stay focused on tasks are the following: Adjust the settings on your cell phone or computer to NOT make noises when people text or e-mail you. Set your phone on airplane mode while with your family; you do it at the movies and you can do it while eating dinner with your loved ones. If you don't have to answer the phone throughout the day, then by all means don't. Leave a message on your phone that says you check your messages at certain times during the day and that you will call them back at given times. Set your Facebook and other social media accounts to not e-mail or text you when someone has posted to your account.

Take Away: We've all become technological turkeys gobbling up information throughout the day. Most people like to communicate many times throughout the day from many places even though it's not necessary. Make sure your web presence is set up to be viewed on mobile devices.

"Timmy, it's Time to Wake Up." If You're Going to Be a Business Owner, Your Actions Must Precede Your Emotions

I was blessed to have my Dad for 50 years before he passed just shy of 80 years. My Dad literally died in my arms, with one of my hands cradling his head and the other gently soothing his forehead with a cool compress. If I had to do it all again, I'd pick him to be my Dad in a heartbeat. He was a quiet man who was married to my mother for 54 years, the father of seven of his own kids and the Dad to at least five other young adults who also called him Dad. The door to my parent's home was always open and there was always enough room at the kitchen table for unexpected guests. My Dad taught me how to throw a curve ball, how to pull the engine in and out of a Chevelle, how to weld, how to fire a shotgun, how to draw a blue print; and through his example, how to act like a gentlemen and how to treat women. He taught me to stand up to bullies, and when necessary, to pop someone in the nose if they were bullying someone else. He taught me the strength of the wolf is the wolf pack and the strength of the wolf pack is the wolf. He also taught me the value of an education and the value of work. I was blessed to have Stephen Louis Hmelar for my Dad.

When I was 12 years old, I remember one morning when my Dad entered my bedroom and gently said, "Timmy, it's time to wake up and get ready to go to work." I felt comfortable in my warm bed and so I replied to my Dad, "Dad I don't feel like getting up and going to work."

To my surprise my Dad walked out of my room and shut the door. I remember being surprised by his reaction and just was about to turn and go back to sleep when my bedroom door once again opened. My father entered my room and said "Timmy, I don't remember walking in your room and saying, 'Timmy would you like to wake up and go to work?' I remember walking in and saying, 'Timmy, it's time to wake up and get ready to go to work.' Now wake up and get ready to go to work." I remember protesting and trying everything to stay in my bed and extend my slumber, but nothing worked. And then my father said, "Timmy, sometimes in life your actions have to precede your emotions. One of the keys to life is acting before you feel like it and then having your emotions catch up to your actions as fast as possible." I will never forget that morning.

Every business owner has to do stuff they don't always feel like doing. I remember once being asked to do a presentation in Chicago at 6:30 AM to Bob Rodgers one of the Presidents of a division of Sears. I was flying into Chicago late the night before my early meeting and knew I wouldn't be getting much sleep. I knew I would have to show up at Sear's headquarters at 5:30 AM local time to double-check that the room's internet access was working and that I could get through Sear's firewall in order for my *preso* to go smoothly. I didn't feel like giving my *preso* at that time, but I did and it rocked. The next thing I knew, I had Bob Rodgers asking me where he should be flying his Learjet to and what time works best for our meeting in Palo Alto. I chuckled and told him to park his Learjet at my private landing strip (San Jose International) and that our meeting would be inconveniently scheduled at 11:30 PM California time - just so he could see what it's like to do business short on sleep. We both laughed and that was the beginning of our working relationship and friendship.

Another memory I have of my childhood had to do with my friends Brad and Matt Mayo. When my family moved from Buffalo, NY to Sherborn, MA, Matt Mayo was the first friend I made in Miss Carpenter's fifth grade class. The Mayo's lived on a dairy and horse farm called Course Brook Farm which was a short walk through the woods from my house. If you've ever worked on a dairy farm or bailed hay, it's a lot of hard work - lots of lifting and long hours. Once you cut hay and bail it you must get it back to the barn. If you leave it out in the rain it will get destroyed and rot and you won't be able to use it in the winter to feed your horses. It doesn't matter if you feel like bailing hay for long hours; if there's rain in the forecast, you suck it up and do whatever it takes to get the job done. Forty years after meeting Matt Mayo we're still friends and I know something about the Mayo brothers - they know the value of work and they know that sometimes your actions have to precede your emotions. It doesn't surprise me at all that to this day that Course Brook Farm not only has survived but is one of the United State's premier places to board your horse or to prepare for national or international horse events.

Take Away: Having the discipline to act before feeling like it is a must if you wish to be successful in life and in business. If you'd rather have a conversation with your pillow than tackling a task that you don't feel like doing - don't go into business for yourself. You will fail. As I committed to writing this book I made the decision to wake up every morning at 5:30 AM and write for an hour and half to complete this book in a timely fashion. I must admit dragging my butt out of bed every morning hasn't always been fun. When I'm tired I just envision my Dad standing next to my bed saying "Timmy, it's time to wake up."

Accounting & Finance

What Color is Your Company Teeter-Tooter? Black or Red? - The Balance Sheet

Most small business owners I know have no idea what their business is worth. Maybe they own some equipment, a couple vehicles, have some inventory, have some accounts receivable and perhaps a building. Maybe they have a note they owe to their parents, have some accounts payable and owe $5,000 on a company credit card. But at the end of the day, they have absolutely no idea what their business is worth.

I like to think of a company's Balance Sheet as a Pinterest or Flickr photo of a business' worth, that is taken on a specific date, and that is then filed away to be used when lenders want to know what your business is worth as you try to secure financing. The world of bean counters has created the Balance Sheet using a simple formula: Assets - Liabilities = Equity (the value of your company).   The key concept is to simply understand that Assets minus Liabilities is equals to Equity. If your Assets are $80,000 and your Liabilities are $60,000, then your Equity is $20,000.

If you've ever bought a home, you probably have created a Personal Balance Sheet. You added up all the cash you had in the bank, added up all the money you had in different IRA's, added up the value of your stock portfolio, went to Kelly Blue Book and figured out the value of your 2006 BMW and the value of your 2008 food stained Chrysler Mini Van. Finally you calculated the equity in your current 1,000 square foot home by subtracting what it would sell for today less what you owe on it. The total of that is your Assets.

Next, you went and calculated all the money you owe people. The $12,000 balance on your student loan, the $18,000 you owe on your hybrid SUV that you bought last year, and the $11,000 you owe to our friends at Visa and American Express. The total of all these expenses is your Liabilities.

By subtracting your liabilities from your assets you were able to calculate your Personal Net Worth. The reason your lender had you prepare a financial statement is because they wanted to know that just in case you have problems paying them back they wanted to make sure you had a secondary source to pay them back. Personal Assets - Personal Liabilities = Personal Net worth.

Balance Sheets, whether personal or business, show the value of you or your business on a given date. If your assets are greater than your liabilities, you have a black teeter tooter - you have a positive net worth or equity in your business. If your liabilities are greater than your assets you have a red teeter tooter - you have a negative net worth and nobody but your closest relatives will lend you a dime.

As a business owner it is important that you understand the purpose and use of a Balance Sheet, and that you have an organized filing system in place so you can calculate a Balance Sheet whenever requested as you seek financing or prepare to sell your business. You should also understand what a P&L is. If you haven't read the chapter *Stop the Bullsh*t! Are You Making*

Money or Not? The Profit & Loss Statement, you should read it now.

If you lack a basic understanding of accounting, you should take an online class or register at your local community college and take a class

in basic accounting. Unless you are planning on opening an accounting business, do not go enroll in a series of accounting classes. Learning the basics should do the trick, just enough for you to get a grip on what is going on. Then, invest in finding a great accountant familiar with your type of business and spend the rest of your time marketing and growing your business.

Take Away: Every company has a company teeter-tooter. You may not go to the local playground and ride the teeter-tooter anymore, but your banker does and he/she has two buckets of paint -- one red and one black. Your banker will analyze your business financial management skills and will paint your company Balance Sheet, your company teeter-tooter, either black or red.

Stop the Bull! Are You Making Money or Not? The Profit & Loss Statement

Unless you're cooking your books, your Profit & Loss Statement (P&L) also called an Income Statement, will tell you if you're making money over a given period of time such as a month, a quarter or year. I like to think of a P&L as a YouTube video of a business' operations for a given period of time, recording all the income and expenses of the business which then tells you if you are making a profit or a loss. Unlike a Balance Sheet, which is the equivalent of a Pinterest financial photograph of your business on a given day and tells you the worth of your company (see *What Color is Your Company Teeter Tooter? Black or Red - The Balance Sheet*), your P&L is NOT normally prepared for a given day.

The P&L's format in its simplest form starts by recording all the money you receive for your company's product or service, then subtracts the costs of making your product or providing your service and comes up with your company's gross profit or loss, then subtracts out your taxes and finally comes up with your company's profit or loss. When I took accounting and finance classes in college, not only did I learn the value of these statements and how to read them, but I also learned it's better to have an accountant manage the recording and assembling of these statements.

When it comes to financial statements, I like to use the analogy of what is important to me when deciding whether to buy a car or truck. How many people will it hold? Can I carry materials or inventory in it? What's my expected gas mileage? And can I tow a trailer? I don't care about what brand of spark plugs it has, I don't care that the tires are Dunlop or Goodyear, and I don't care that it takes 10W-30 oil. I want to be able to look at the gauges on my dashboard and make decisions about how I drive my car. Just like I use the gauges on my car to make driving decisions I use the information in my financial statements to make decisions on how I drive my business. I know my car has a master cylinder for the brakes, I know it has a water pump, radiator, power steering and a battery, but I don't spend time focusing on them on a daily basis. When my mechanics Chuck or Jamie, who inspects my car on a regular basis, tell me the tires are worn, the fan belt is cracked or my brake light is out, I listen to their advice and normally have him fix the problem. Chuck of *CMK Automotive or Jamie of Sherman's Automotive* are the equivalent to my car as John of *A to Z Accounting* is to my accounting. Chuck, Jamie and John know the big stuff and small stuff about my car or company's books. I let them do what they do best while I focus on driving my car as a tool to make money.

Before you go out and become an accountant or mechanic, I suggest the following. First, learn the basics of accounting from online resources or your local community college. Do not spend hours and hours mastering the minutiae of constructing financial statements. Get the basics and have the ability to read your P&L and Balance Sheet. Second, hire an accountant you trust, you like and who understands your kind of business. John Zukoski, the accountant for my construction business knows the operations of construction businesses inside out. Third, have your accountant set up the specific accounts to be used in your business for bookkeeping. And finally, have your accountant prepare reports and tax returns for you as data points for you to manage your business.

Finally, I suggest you buy a copy of *It's How Much You Keep That Counts! Not What you Make* by Ronald Mueller. I had the opportunity of meeting Ronald many years ago and found him to be extremely informed about small business management and even more so, specifically about different deductions and expenses that the IRS allows. If you ever have the opportunity to hear Ronald talk, it's well worth your time. He's a gifted speaker with lots of funny and entertaining anecdotes about small business and business expenses.

Take Away: Your Profit and Loss Statement doesn't lie. For a given time period, it will tell you if you're making money or not. And, if you're more interested in preparing your company's financial statements or changing the oil in your car instead of marketing and growing your business, maybe you should go work for H & R Block or Jiffy Lube.

What's in Your Garden - Kiwis, Tomatoes or Oak Trees? Cash Flow is King

I hate the way tomatoes taste. I never eat them with my salad or put them on a burger. In fact, I think somewhere in my youth I vaguely remember having a tomato fight with my brother Frank who used to have an arm like Rodger Clemons. I think the last time I ate a tomato, I was eleven years old and it was inserted in my mouth by my brother at approximately 70 mph. But here's the ironic thing about me and tomatoes, when it comes to business and managing money I view myself as a tomato farmer. This was a lesson that took me 25 years to learn.   Cash flow is king. Without personal and business cash flow, your business will fail. One more time -- without personal and business cash flow, your business will fail. Let me explain.

Tomato Farming

Everyone needs money to survive on a daily basis. You need to have the ability to create an income stream quickly that is predictable – just like a gardener knows growing tomatoes is relatively easy to do and they grow fast.   Every successful entrepreneur needs to eat, have a roof over their head, must be able to move from point A to point B and have some cash to meet minimum daily personal and business expenses. Tomato Farming is the concept that as an entrepreneur the most important cash management step you need to take is to have

CASH FLOW.   You must have a source of income to cover your daily personal and business expenses. Sources of income to cover your daily expenses can be from your savings or from a job that you hold while starting your business. Or maybe you're one of those talented people able to raise money from other people – most likely a family member, friend or possibly and angle investor or venture capitalist. - The point is you figure out a way to meet your daily personal and business expenses. You have a garden of tomatoes.

It doesn't matter how many customers you have or what the size of your accounts receivable are - if you don't figure out how to meet your daily cash flow needs your business will fail, your kids won't get to go to an Ivy League College, your electricity will be shut off, and you will see the tail lights of your significant other's car as he/she drives off to a different financial future. Before opening the door to your business make sure you plant your tomato garden first and make sure you have CASH FLOW that comes to you fast and in small doses - just like tomatoes growing in a garden.

Oak Tree Farming

Oak tree farmers invest for the long run and every oak tree farmer has a tomato garden spinning off cash to meet daily expenses. Oak tree farmers tend to be moderate risk takers and put their money in safe, time proven investments like the stock market or real estate. Oak tree farmers have figured out how to meet their daily financial needs while salting away money for a rainy day and for a bleak future if/when the U.S. goes broke and can't meet the pension and medical needs of its citizens. However, some Oak tree farmers are also Kiwi farmers. These are the people who have diligently planned their finances and have some extra cash to go to Las Vegas with. However, most kiwi farmers don't have an oak tree farm.

Kiwi Farming

Kiwi farmers are the dreamers. They are the technologists, the innovators, the entrepreneurs who mostly see the world through rose colored glasses. They put a unique spin on the business world and take financial risks far greater than playing poker in Las Vegas. Some famous and successful kiwi farmers are Bob Noyce founder of Intel, Steve Jobs of Apple, Mark Zuckerberg of Facebook and Bob Parsons of GoDaddy.com. Most kiwi farmers are failures, unknown faces to the world that believed in their idea and ended up losing lots of money, lots of time and maybe a family member or two.

Business Person Take Away: If you have the next great idea that will change the world, make sure you have sufficient cash flow for you and the business to live. Without daily cash flow you will fail.

Farmer Take Away: Before you plant kiwis, plant lots of tomatoes and plant a couple of oak trees.

Health & Fitness

Fat Man Skinny Man - Meet Thunder Thighs Exercise and Business Success

True Story.

> I have a friend Ed. Ed is in his late 40's, is about 5'7", and weighs about 140 pounds. Recently Ed went to the doctor for his physical check-up and found out he had gained 4 lbs in the last year. What happened next shocked Ed. Ed's doctor told him he was worried about Ed's weight. Ed was starting to become the all too common "Fat Man Skinny Man." You know, the guy who is thin except in his gut. You know, the Buddha Body. The doctor explained that if Ed continued to gain 4 lbs/year he would be obese in just 5 years time. Ed was advised to start exercising on a daily basis and alter his eating habits. Ed took his doctor's advice and incorporated a fitness program into his lifestyle.

Okay guys, wanna know if you're a Fat Man Skinny Man or if you're on your way to becoming a Buddha Body? Here's the test I use to monitor my weight. I don't need a doctor to tell me I need to lose weight. All I do is look down at my belt buckle. When I look down at my belt buckle if I can't see my belt or if the top of my belt buckle is sticking out further than the bottom of the buckle, I know I have the body of a Fat Man Skinny Man.

Then I know that my exercise and eating habits are not right. I need to make a change.

Another true story.

> Donna, a college classmate of mine, used to tell me about her exercise struggles and how she wanted to get rid of her "Thunder Thighs". She would wear a black hoodie and loose fitting sweat pants, and begrudgingly go to the gym in an effort to lose weight. She knew she was overweight and she didn't want people to see her figure. She was a member of the Thunder Thighs Club and wanted out. With some hard work and re-programming her mind about fitness and diet, Donna was able to change her figure. In fact she was so successful with her new fitness habits that she lost over 100 lbs and went on to become a tri-athlete. She finally quit the Thunder Thighs Club and hasn't been a member for over 20 years. If you own some sweats that you wear to hide your figure sounds like you're a member of the Thunder Thighs. You too need to make a change.

So what's all this talk about Fat Man Skinny Man and Thunder Thighs have to do with my business? Everything. Studies show that people who are fit tend to be happier than unfit people. They tend to have less stress, are more productive at work and are able to focus and keep their energy level high. On the other hand, unfit and overweight people take more sick days than fit people, are more likely to develop diabetes, hypertension or heart disease, are more likely to have strokes and more likely to have high cholesterol. All these are bad for you especially if you're planning on managing your business as you get older.

It's hard to do business transactions if you're dead or you're incapable of working.

Dr. Travis Stork, co-host of the TV show *The Doctors*, writes in his book *The Lean Belly Prescription* "*When patients arrive in the ER, I have literally a few seconds to decide on what's wrong and how I can help.*

Guess which vital sign I check first? Their weight. The most important indicator of how people will manage a health crisis is how much belly fat they're carrying. Why? Because your health risks climb right along with your waist measurement. Not only are high levels of belly fat associated with heart disease, diabetes, stroke, and cancer, but obese patients are also 37% more likely to die from injuries sustained in a car accident."

I found the best way for me to stay fit is to have an accountability partner - someone to share my fitness path with. Efi Luzon, John Thompson and Eric Schuur are three of my friends that I share my love of jogging with. Funny thing about my jogging buddies is they're all incredibly successful at business. Efi is one of the nation's leading commercial real estate agents; John Thompson is co-founder of Intero Real Estate Services, one of the nation's fastest growing real estate brokerages; and Eric has been incredibly successful in the field of science. We run together, we share our life experiences together, and we all know that fit people are more productive than unfit people.

I have two other health/fitness accountability partners on Facebook – Donnamarie Amara Tizzano and Michelle Brown. Both are extremely passionate about fitness and life. Donnamarie is an old high school friend and Michelle is someone I met through John Thompson, one of my realtor friends. I find by following them on FB and by communicating with them I always feel turbo-charged and more focused and determined to stay fit.

Take Away: Want to climb the company or business ladder to success? Get an accountability fitness partner and literally take your first steps.   Be fit, get healthy, and soon you'll be climbing your ladder to success two rungs at a time. This way, you'll achieve your business success faster and you'll be able to enjoy it longer.

If You Want Your Dreams to Come True, Try Getting Some Sleep and put down your can of 5-Hour Energy Drink

If you're a typical American, you are not getting enough sleep. Most people need eight hours of sleep per night and most people aren't getting enough. I don't know how many cans of 5-Hour Energy Drink I see people drinking in an effort to overcome their lack of sleep and energy. Some people are fine with less than 8 hours per night and others need more than 8 hours per night. I typically go to bed around 9PM and wake up at 5AM. All my friends, family and business colleagues know that I don't attend meetings that run after 8PM. I've learned that after 8PM, I can't focus on the task at hand and therefore I've decided to let people know I do not participate in meetings at a less than peak performance level due to my body being sleepy. It's not fair to me and it's not fair to my biz colleagues.

 "If you HOOT with the OWLS at NIGHT, you CAN'T SOAR with the EAGLES at DAWN!"

- Anonymous

Different people have different sleeping patterns. We all tend to categorize ourselves as either "night owls" or "morning people." Until the last couple of hundred years, the majority of humans have been "morning people" who were awake during the day and asleep when it's dark. Simply put, the sun was necessary for the majority of human's to hunt and gather food. All that has changed now and very few people are involved in the production of food. For those of you who work their ass off during the week, and then in an effort to catch up on their sleep, oversleep on the weekends -- your lack of sleep during the week is hurting your body. Your body knows when it has been sleep deprived and takes a cumulative beating from it. If you choose to temporarily abuse your body by not sleeping enough, a short cat nap can help to temporarily help your body's sleep needs. The key here is to not repeatedly abuse your body by not getting enough sleep.

Humans have thrived by using the free light offered by the sun and have benefited physically and psychologically from getting enough sleep and spending time in the sunlight. If you don't want to go to your local GNC Vitamin Store to buy vitamin D, try getting out in the sun. Sunlight offers your body a free dose Vitamin D. What's so important about Vitamin D? Vitamin D helps your body keep its bones and heart strong, helps keep your immune system boosted, it releases melatonin which is a hormone that helps regulates your body's sleep, it helps fight heart disease, reduces bad cholesterol and even helps the body produce more insulin which in turn helps turn the sugar glucose into energy.

"Sleep is the golden chain that ties health and our bodies together."

Thomas Dekker

Take Away: Some time in our life, all of us have experienced a lack of sleep where we've all felt testy and irritable. Most people have also had someone apologize to them for treating them poorly due to their lack of sleep and anxiousness. If you're trying to launch a new business or are busting your ass on a short term project, I understand how your drive is temporarily overriding your body's need for sleep. The problem starts when the lack of sleep lifestyle, becomes entrenched and a way of life. So if you want your dreams to come true, if you don't want to be irritable with others, if you don't want to have all kinds of diseases, start getting 8 hours of sleep per night. Sweet dreams.

Social Media

Is Facebook a Big Time Suck? Are You A Facebook Junkie?

Joke: Facebook (FB) Consultant to Business Owner

> Want to know how to make more money with Facebook? Stop dicking around all day on Facebook posting pictures and personal quotes regarding your psychological shortcomings and try going out and banging on customer doors. Now give me $500 and have a great business day!

Many business owners would be financially better off if they followed the advice above and paid the five hundred dollars. They simply lack the control to focus on the activities that matter most to growing and managing their business. Yes, it feels good to know what your high school buddies are up to, who's in Cabo San Lucas sucking down margaritas like a camel preparing to cross the desert, and which one of your psycho ex-lovers just posted a photo of themselves keying their current significant others car writing "Cheating Whore or Bastard" on the side of their new $50,000 SUV. But at the end of the day the big question is, "Did this help grow my business and make some company profits?"

For many business owners FB is nothing more than a time toilet. Time flushed away never to be given back. Other business owners understand the power of FB and how to use it to grow their business. These are the business people who use FB as a marketing tool – a marketing tool that can create visibility, credibility, convertibility and profitability (if you haven't read the chapter Does Your Business have Ibility you should read it after this chapter) for their business.

FB is not in existence because Mark Zuckerberg is a giving, loving philanthropist trying to make the world a better place. FB is in business to make money. Zuckerberg's job is to make money for the shareholders of FB. If Zuckerberg is like most successful entrepreneurs I've met (FYI, I've never met Mark Zuckerberg), he's trying to make money and make the world a better place at the same time. So how does FB make money? Why, it is simply by showing business people how to market their product or service to other FB members. FB is really a lead generation tool for business people to get other FB users into a sales funnel.

According to recent statistics, approximately 1.2 billion people have FB accounts and according to HubSpot (one of my favorite businesses that I follow on FB), 43% of business selling to other businesses and 77% of businesses selling to consumers have acquired a client using FB. I don't know how many FB profiles are aliases or are the same people creating multiple accounts or how many are actual business accounts. However, I do know that a lot of people have at least taken the time to explore FB and create a profile. I look at FB as a huge high school reunion, family reunion, my softball team, block party, client appreciation event, business networking event and rave rolled into one big event. Where there are lots of people I smell a good time and I smell money. With that many people on FB, the clever business people, have figured out how to use it to grow their business.

Some ways I use FB to grow my business is by providing useful information to existing and prospective clients who follow my FB business page. I answer their questions, announce upcoming events and take polls to help me know what my business' followers want. I have a strategy for FB and I don't spend endless hours mindlessly surfing FB. Not that I disapprove of socializing with your buddies, I'm just saying that there are better ways on when and how to do it.

If you're smart and want to maximize the power of Facebook for growing your business, go to www.facebook.com/HubSpot, LIKE the HubSpot page, scroll through their page and download the HubSpot's free e-book *How to Master Facebook Marketing in 10 Days*. I can't think of a better book to kick start your business' FB campaign and save you time and money.

<u>Take Away:</u> Don't be a Facebook junkie wasting your hours away. Just like Mark Zuckerberg did; you can use Facebook to make the world a better place and make money at the same time. Got a question about Facebook? Go to Facebook.com/weblunchbox like the page and I'll do my best to answer your questions.

Monologues are for David Letterman, Chelsea Handler, Jon Stewart & Conan O'Brien; Dialogues are for Small Business Owners

I hardly ever stay up past 10 PM. When I do stay up late and watch TV, I'm always amazed on how the different talk show hosts all start their respective shows with a clever monologue spewing out their own twisted version of the past week's most current events and gossip. Most of the time their one-way verbal diarrhea is funny, sometimes hilarious, sometimes in poor taste and sometimes just sucks and isn't funny at all. Regardless of how well their monologues are received, it really takes big balls to go out there and have a one-way conversation in front of millions of people in hope that they find it funny and that they won't change the station.

Successful business people, on the contrary, are not comedians spewing out monologues. Successful business people have big ears and small mouths. They are engaged with their customers and have dialogues with their customers on a regular basis. Not listening to your customers can be devastating to your business which means that it can also destroy your personal finances and retirement along the way.

Years ago, my brother Frank and I were hired as subcontracted finish carpenters to work on Carlie Fiorini's house, who at that time was the CEO of Hewlett Packard. At the end of the project I gave a Customer Feedback Questionnaire to Paul Keenan, the Site Superintendent for R.J. Daily (the builder) asking for his feedback. The questionnaire had seven questions rating our work on a scale of 1-5, five being the highest. This could be answered in less than one minute. I'll never forget Paul Keenan's response of disbelief that someone in the construction industry would actually want to know how to improve their company's services. To this day, Paul Keenan still hires my brother Frank as a subcontracted contractor to work on the homes of some of the richest people in the world.

The Customer Feedback Questionnaire

As a business owner, you don't have to spend hundreds, or even thousands, of dollars in developing a Customer Feedback Questionnaire. Ask the following seven basic questions, have your customer answer them on a scale from 1-5 with 1 being extremely dissatisfied and 5 being extremely satisfied. You can use the template below for your own, but just make sure you substitute your company's product or service in the questionnaire that follows. You can also create your own set of questions depending on what is applicable for your business. Key point here is to make the questionnaire easy and quick to complete.

1. Are you happy with the quality of the product or service you received?

2. Are you happy with the pricing of the product or service?

3. Are you happy with the time frame for the product or service you received?

4. Are you happy with the way communication issues were handled?

5. Were the workers professional and polite?

6. Would you recommend this business to others without hesitation?

7. Comments or Suggestion on how to improve our company services?

*Yelp: If you write reviews on Yelp, your comments would be greatly appreciated.

At the end of the Customer Feedback Questionnaire, I personally sign the form and give it to the client with a pre-addressed return envelope.

Take Away: If you want your business to survive and maximize its value, you need to listen to your customers constantly and engage in a dialogue with them often. Acting like Jay Leno delivering his nightly monologue may be fun, but it can get your in business trouble, as your potential clients run to your competitor who is more like Oprah Winfrey.

Hallelujah Brothers and Sistas - Who wants to testify? People Don't Trust Corporate Advertising – People Trust Yelp

Who do you trust more? A happy customer who has purchased a product and can't stop raving about it or a slick corporate website or advertisement trying to manipulate you into buying the same product? Who do you trust more? An unhappy customer who has purchased a product and is pissed off and regrets their purchasing decision or a slick corporate website or advertisement trying to manipulate you into buying the same product? People trust Yelp!

Yelp is a website/social media platform that lets people share their purchasing experiences. The good, the bad, the delicious, the poor service, the friendly staff, the great guacamole, the cold soup, the waiter who doesn't give a damn and whatever else people find worthy of posting. You name it its on Yelp.

Let's say you're traveling to Palo Alto and want to find a Mexican restaurant. As I'm writing right now I'm literally on Yelp entering, Mexican food, Palo Alto, CA in the search boxes at the top of the page. Let's see, at the top of the page is some place called Café Del Sol which shows up in a slightly pink shaded box with small text in the upper right corner saying Yelp Ad (this is a paid ad to be placed at the top of the page). I don't like this and I don't trust this first ad because the business has paid Yelp to be placed at the top of the page. I just don't trust paid advertising. Just below the paid ad is Palo Alto Sol, a restaurant that 382 people have reviewed with an average score of three and half stars out of five. No pink shaded box, Palo Alto Sol has not paid to be on the Yelp platform. I like this.

Something very important to know about Yelp is that if your business doesn't have a profile on Yelp your customers can start the profile without your consent. Just because you didn't create a Yelp profile doesn't mean you don't have one. An important thing to do is to go to Yelp and enter your business name and city and see if you're already on Yelp. If you haven't created a Yelp profile you should do it now. If you find you have a Yelp profile that you didn't create you should click on the words that say "Work Here? Unlock this Business Page". Once you've clicked on the link you will be contacted by Yelp to make sure that you actually are the business owner and then you will be able to respond to the people who have reviewed your business and add more features to your company profile.

Got a Yelp profile and got an unhappy Yelper blasting your business? If possible, the best way to handle unhappy Yelp reviewers is to do it in public on your Yelp profile. Don't ignore negative comments, as it tends to show you don't give a damn about your customers. If you need help responding to a Yelper slamming your business make sure you read the chapter "Do Your Barbequing in the Back Yard" – Don't let Your Business Get Barbequed on Yelp.

A huge controversary involving Yelp is that many small business owners claim that Yelp keeps bad reviews on their company profile and removes positive reviews unless you switch to a paid

Yelp profile. I don't know how Yelp writes its algorithms for managing reviews but I've heard from many, many business owners that they think Yelp is trying to extort money from them. I've also read in the newspaper and online that there have been class action lawsuits against Yelp and every single lawsuit has been dismissed.

Take Away: Don't underestimate the power of Yelp. Consumers trust testimonials from strangers more that paid advertisements. When you manage your Yelp profile do it in a friendly and transparent manner allowing readers to feel a positive psychological connection with your business.

Do Your Barbecuing in the Backyard, Don't Let Your Business get barbequed on YELP

I like to barbeque with my family and friends. Like many American families, we have a rundown black grill in the backyard that is hard to get a fire started and has little gnarly looking cooking tools that seem to mysteriously run off into the night and can't be found for days. Despite the necessary gymnastics of getting the fire started, we enjoy barbequing enough that we even barbeque food during the winter months. At my home I'm the one who always does the barbequing. Just as I have a plan for managing my family barbequing you should have a plan for managing your Yelp profile.

Just like the many hours I've spent barbequing in the backyard, I've spent many hours with business owners helping them manage their Yelp account. I've seen business owners have their Yelp profile high jacked by a competitor. I've met many business owners who've never claimed their Yelp profile (they've never clicked on their Yelp profile and let Yelp know they are the business owner which would allow them to manage their business profile and respond to the comments made by customers) and I've seen many businesses receive incredibly poor reviews from pissed off customers where the business owner never responded to the poor review.

The sad part is that most of these business owners have done nothing to manage their Yelp profile. It's like they know they have a grill in their backyard, that they've got some hamburgers on the grill and they forgot to check on the food grilling away which eventually gets burned and dried out only to have their guest tell them how the food sucks and tastes like something found in a bag of charcoal.

True Story. This past week I was sitting in one of my newly opened offices - okay I was sitting at a table at *Saratoga Bagels* in Saratoga, California eating a blueberry bagel with low-fat strawberry cream cheese, borrowing a cubicle (actually a table), using their free Wifi and borrowing some electricity and heat all for the cost of my yummy bagel. I met Mei, the owner who told me that she made the "best bagels", and that she knew I would love my bagel. We shared small talk and I asked Mei *"What should I do if you don't make the best bagels? What if she made the world's best bagels?"* I told Mei that if she made the world's best bagels, I would go to Yelp and write her a great review. What happened next didn't surprise me, but Mei experienced a Yelp epiphany.

For starters, I'm not an expert on bagels. I had never been to *Saratoga Bagels* before last week and my main concern in choosing to enter Saratoga Bagels was because it had free Wifi and an open table for me to sit down for a couple of hours to work on this book. Mei is short and I could barely see the top of her head from behind the counter full of all different kind of bagels. When I picked the blueberry bagel, it was Mei who suggested I try it with low-fat strawberry cream cheese. Mei was right, she did make the best bagels, and I was right because to me it tasted like the world's best bagel. I went to Yelp to write my review and the first thing I noticed Mei had never claimed her Yelp profile as the business owner.

I went back to the counter and asked Mei why she hadn't claimed her Yelp business profile. She looked at me funny, not knowing whether I was a scammer, a jerk salesmen or just a friendly person trying to help her out. When I explained to her I had helped hundreds of small businesses with social media management and that she had many great reviews and a couple of so-so reviews, she told me she had never visited her Yelp profile. I then let Mei know if she had the time and was interested, I could explain to her some stuff about Yelp. A couple of minutes later I was joined by my new friend and we spent some time looking at her Yelp profile.

I told Mei that she must claim her Yelp profile and explained to her how her customers had created a Yelp profile for her business. I showed her that she had 83 reviews to date and her average Yelp score was four and a half stars out of five. I told her things looked quite good but that if I were she I would claim the page and respond to the people reviewing her business. Especially I would respond to the people who had given her business less than a four star review.

I gave her the following example. A Yelper by the name of David L. came to *Saratoga Bagels* on August 6, 2012 and shared his experience on Yelp. He shared that he bought a Lox Omelette for $6.49 that was *"Mediocre", had a lot more egg than lox (smoked salmon) and overall I really didn't like the taste."* and later on David L. went on to end his review by writing *"Service was good. However, a fly flew in the open door and got into the bagel counter."*

I suggested Mei responded to David L. in the following way after she had claimed her Yelp profile.

> *"Hey David. Thanks for your feedback about my business. I'm sorry to hear you didn't think you received value for your Lox Omelette. Please come back to* Saratoga Bagel*, tell anyone at the counter that you're David L. and I guarantee you will receive a FREE Lox Omelette smothered in Lox to your heart's desire. As far as that bagel-crazed kamikaze fly is concerned I am pretty sure he no longer inhibits planet earth. Looking forward to seeing you again. Mei."*

The key here is to address the Yelper's review head on and in public. Be courteous, don't be offensive, be light-hearted, and be sincere. If you screwed up, admit it, take responsibility (unless the reviewer is an obvious scammer and psychopath) and offer a refund or replacement. Do whatever it takes to make your customer happy. If you do this, other Yelpers visiting your company profile will see that there's a real business person who cares enough about his customers to actually take the time to address their complaints and learn from the experience. I'm hoping Mei follows my advice and makes David L. a raving fan of her business.

Take Away: Successful business people barbeque in the backyard and not on Yelp. Use Yelp to communicate with your customers in a two-way dialogue that benefits your customers and your business. Also, if you're in Saratoga, California and feel the urge for a bagel, stop in to *Saratoga Bagel*, order a blueberry bagel with low-fat strawberry cream cheese and tell Mei I said hello. And if you happen to go to Yelp and find that

Mei still hasn't claimed her Yelp page yet, tell her I said to hop on it.

You've Seen the Movie Avatar - But Where's Your Gravatar?

When I think of the movie Avatar, the James Cameron movie released in 2009, a head shot image of a bluish colored creature that looks like a cross between a human and the pink panther comes into my mind. Although I liked the movie Avatar, I like gravatars even more. What the heck is a gravatar? Why should I have one? And what does it do for my business?

So what's a gravatar? Gravatar stands for globally recognized avatar. A gravatar is a square shaped image that gives a visual image of you or your business when you post or comment on someone's blog or forum. A gravatar can be a photo of you, a cartoon character, your company logo or anything that can be drawn graphically. In order for your gravatar to show up with your posts, you must have first created a gravatar on the gravatar website. Take note, your gravatar will only show up when you make a comment where you also need to enter your e-mail. Creating a gravatar only takes a few minutes and is free. To create a gravatar go to www.gravatar.com.

According to a search I just did on Google on how many people read blogs in the United States, it appears that somewhere between 100 - 239 million people do. Depending on what you believe, that's approximately 25% - 77% of the population reading blogs. Remember a blog is a website where people can simply post articles, photos or videos for the entire world to see. Also, most blogs allow people to respond and make comments. My favorite blog is Monday Morning Mojo written by Tom Tognoli.

Creating a gravatar is a great way to brand your business. When most people read comments on blogs or forums, they have a hard time associating a comment with any person or business. Knowing people are visual creatures and that they prefer to look at images instead of text, this should be all you need to know that creating a gravatar is a must. If you haven't read You Might Not Be Square, But Your Logo Should Be: Tips for Designing Your Company Logo, you should do it now.

Gravatars are only square shaped and if you design it wrong or with too many pixels (gravatars are only 80 by 80 pixels), your image may get altered when trying to use it as a gravatar. If you haven't created a gravatar and you post to a blog without it, you will meet the gravatar mystery man. The gravatar mystery man is a grey and white caricature silhouette of a person. He's boring and stands out like a white bunny in a snow storm at the North Pole.

So how does my gravatar end up with my posts? Blogs have plug-ins (special programs) that when they see an e-mail appear the blog knows to go to the gravatar website and see if there is a gravatar associated with that e-mail. If you have a gravatar it shows up with your post. If you don't have a gravatar its time for the grey and white mystery man to take front and center.

Take Away: Be *"Younique"* with your business and create a *gravatar* that will show up when you make comments on blogs or forums. It's a must for branding your business and before you go watch a re-run of Avatar, make sure your business has a *gravatar*.

Boxers, Briefs or Commando - Automating & Syndicating Social Media Content from Anywhere, Any Time in Your Underwear

Boxers, Briefs or Commando? I wear boxers. I don't like the way briefs feel and I'm too afraid of a horrible accident involving a zipper to go commando. Why the heck am I talking about underwear? I'm talking about underwear because you can manage your social media campaign from anyplace, anytime and it doesn't matter if you're wearing underwear or not. Why? As long as you have internet access, the whole process can be automated and scheduled using tools like WordPress and HootSuite.

A typical week for me at Web Lunch Box involves training 10-15 small business owners in setting up their social media campaign, consulting with another 2-3 small businesses on a one-on-one basis, managing the Web Lunch Box social media campaign and usually one public speaking engagement. One comment I hear almost daily is that I don't have time to manage my business' social media campaign. My belief is that once the appropriate tools such as a WordPress, Facebook Business Page, Twitter account, YouTube Channel, LinkedIn Profile, Yelp and other misc. small biz listing sites such as Google Places are set up, the whole social media campaign can be managed in 30-60 minutes/day. If you haven't read the chapter *Do You Have the Gift of Gab? Or Do You Have Big Balls? Marketing vs. Sales,* you should hop on it. It is my firm belief that the most important activity of any business is marketing. Another interesting observation I've made is that it's the same small business owners complaining they don't have time to market their company using social media who aren't making the income level they desire.

A cool thing about the WordPress blog platform is that the interface includes a simple-to-use Posting Options Tab allowing the author to schedule when the post is published and to which social media sites. I can schedule when to post the blog article I've just written; the date and time, or I can enter "in 5 days", or I can enter "in 2 hours" - it's really that simple. The other cool thing is I can select auto-post and have my blogs automatically post to my Facebook Business Page, Twitter, other blogs, or YouTube. I also have the option of selecting which other sites I manually want to have my blogs posted to. The important thing to remember is the more often you post unique content on a regular basis to different social media sites the higher your business tends to rank on Google, Yahoo and Bing. One caveat about using auto-post is that you can end up pissing off people if you post too much content, too often over too many social media sites.

HootSuite is a great tool for writing updates and posting them to Twitter, Facebook and other sites. In order to use HootSuite you must have a Twitter account. Just like WordPress allows you to schedule and syndicate blog posts, HootSuite allows you to make posts using the Twitter interface, and even upload photos and videos to multiple sites very easily. Simply go to HootSuite.com and in minutes you can have your HootSuite account set up and you'll be able to sit down and write all your automated and syndicated posts for the week in one sitting.

Two major netiquette errors I see often are: first, posting Tweets and Facebook updates to peoples LinkedIn accounts. In my opinion, LinkedIn is for business networking and answering business questions. It is not the place to post quotes and interrupt professional people's daily lives. The other major snafu I see is when people use sites like Foursquare and Facebook Places and continually post to their social media accounts where they are.

True Story: I once had a successful realtor in Los Angeles continually send me his FourSquare updates to my Facebook Business Page. I'm talking 10-12 updates/day. I sent a private message to this realtor asking him to stop sending me updates on his whereabouts and he replied that he had paid someone to set up and connect his social media accounts and he didn't know how to disconnect the syndicated feeds. After one more day of receiving numerous updates about where he was eating a burrito or drinking a mojito, I hid his posts from my wall and no longer see any of his posts. Don't be a Barney and spam people with unwanted information.

Jurgen Weller, a good friend of mine, uses HootSuite to stay in touch with the nearly 5,000 followers he has on Facebook. I'm amazed by how many people think Jurgen spends all day on Facebook making updates when in reality he uses HootSuite to schedule his updates giving the appearance that he's doing nothing but sitting in his office screwing around on Facebook. Jurgen uses HootSuite to make two scheduled posts to his Facebook personal account each day. One post in the morning usually involves a funny quote or humorous story he wants to share; the second post in the afternoon is about professional/personal development. On Friday evenings, Jurgen posts his "Romantic Fridays" post about some kind of fun thing to do with your special significant other with a sexual twist to it.

Take Away: It doesn't matter if you wear boxers, briefs, a *tanga* or go commando. To be an efficiency expert with your posts, use tools that allow you to schedule and syndicate your social media presence. And if you're trying to spice up your sex life on Friday evenings, check out Jurgen Weller's Romantic Fridays.

Sit or Squat - How Charmin Toilet Paper Keeps Their Brand On Your Mind and On Your Bottom!   The Power of Mobile Apps

We've all been there!   It's not fun and can be downright embarrassing.   And it comes at the most inopportune time. Whether stuck in a traffic jam, walking through a park with your five year old, or on your first date with the person of your dreams - Mother Nature comes calling with the furry of a Tsunami rainstorm or like Mount Vesuvious getting ready to erupt.   If you're sitting in the passenger's seat of your friends car, you cross your legs and bite your nails; or if you're walking from the train station down University Avenue in Palo Alto on the way to your office at Starbucks, your walk probably resembles a cross between the chicken dance at a Greek wedding and the Macarena after consuming five shots of Tequila.   What do you do now?   You thank Charmin Toilet Paper's spokesperson Mr. Whipple and Apple's Steve Jobs of course!

You whip out your smart phone, press the *Sit or Squat* app and find there's a restroom in Pizza My Heart located at the corner of University Avenue and Emerson Street.   You try to walk in a non-hurried fashion praying that the bathroom door is not locked.

After the blissful release of Mother Nature's horrific calling, you gather your thoughts and re-assemble your self-esteem and hit the streets with your self-confidence in check and the kick back in your walk. But what really just happened? Your good friends at Charmin Toilet Paper just saved your ass (pun intended) by creating a mobile app and having it available for free at the App Store on iTunes, the Android Market on your Droid phone, and at the App World on your Blackberry. By creating the Sit or Squat app, Charmin Toilet Paper is subtly making a brand impression on you outside the aisle of your local super market. It's clever and since it's now estimated there are more searches being conducted on smart phones and iPads than desktops, it's a must for businesses to be where their customers are when they need them. That place is on their mobile phone.

Interested in creating your own app and don't know where to start, and don't have a lot of money? Check out Shoutem.com. The founders of Shoutem have gone out of their way to make creating your own app relatively simple. Another great source of current info and tools for maximizing your business' online presence is Mashable.com. I love Mashable's content and even follow them on Facebook.

Take away: Help your customers even when they're not making a purchase of your product or service. You can provide value to your customer's lives and keep your brand on their mind (and bottom) even when your customer's aren't making a purchase. Your customers are on mobile devices and so should your business. BTW, if you ever use Sit and Squat and find the bathroom located at Seale Park in Palo Alto, CA you can thank me, Tim Hmelar, your social media evangelist and Sit and Squat bathroom site contributor. Gotta Run!

Don't be "The Missing Link - 5 Action Items to Turbo Charge Your LinkedIn Business Profile

"Not embracing social media is like writing on the cave walls after Gutenberg invented the printing press." ~ dotJenna

Almost every business person has heard of LinkedIn — the Mountain View, CA social media powerhouse where professionals network and people seeking employment go to get themselves a job. In my experience working with small business owners I have found that the majority of small business owners DON'T KNOW that they can build a profile for their company on LinkedIn.

LinkedIn is the world's largest social networking site for professionals where they can share professional information and look for new careers. If you wish to gain the most from your LinkedIn profile you should implement the following five items so that Google crawls better your LinkedIn profile.

1. Create a custom URL for your business on LinkedIn. Google likes domain names that include the name of the business or product. Once you've built your LinkedIn biz page, make sure you make multiple pages on your profile for the different products or services you offer.

2. Put relevant keywords and bold them at the top of your Business LinkedIn profile.

2. Put relevant **keywords** and **bold them** at the top of your **Business LinkedIn profile.**

See the BIG DIFFERENCE between my two number 2 items here. One poops, **one pops**.

3. Put your recommendations section at the top of your profile. I've found most people don't give a flying monkey's butt about where you went to school and how many awards you won while in college. Prospective customers want to know how many happy customers you have and what they say about you. Remember, social media is about helping others and is NOT about YOU! It's easy to move your recommendations section up in your profile by simply clicking on the recommendations header and dragging it up to the top of your profile.

4. Have a picture in your profile - people like to see people. Be smart - show yourself doing your business activity or in front of something that brands your business. And oh yeah, don't forget to smile.

5. Participate in discussions and groups. Ivan Misner, the founder of BNI (Business Networking International - the world's largest belly button to belly button networking group) says "Givers Gain." If you participate on a regular basis in online discussions and groups, you soon give others confidence that you're an expert in your field and a Good Joe.

Take Away: Don't be the missing link because in reality, there are no missing links. Somebody will kick your ass in business if you don't seize the moment when it arises. Carpe diem

Curry Up Now: Roach Coaches, and The Marriage of Old School Marketing with Social Media Marketing

Roach Coach? Indian Street Food? Softball? Facebook? Twitter? Social Media? huh? First let me address one thing up front; when I use the term "Roach Coach", I'm using the term to describe a mobile catering/food truck. I have no disrespect for anyone who operates one of these catering businesses. As a small business owner and geek, the first thing I think of when I hear the words Mobile Marketing is some kind of cell phone technology that either makes my shopping experience easier or a technology that tries to get my contact info in an effort to manipulate my buying behavior. *Curry Up Now*, no, not Hurry Up Now, turned everything upside down with my definition of mobile marketing this past Tuesday.

I play softball almost every Tuesday in a co-ed adult softball league in Palo Alto for a team called "More Fun Than Bowling." This past Tuesday as I pulled into the parking lot at Greer Park, I saw this huge orange and red food truck parked in the parking lot with a swarm of people sitting on the ground near the truck eating, socializing, laughing and joking. At first I didn't think much of it until a guy named Blake walked up to me and said that his team Intapp (Intapp makes software for the legal community) was inviting our team to join his team for a dinner of Indian food from the truck in the parking lot after the game.

My first thought was *"What? Free food? From a 'roach coach'?"* What the heck is this guy smoking? After thanking Blake I went up to the home plate umpire and jokingly told him that if our team started to get sick and puke on the field it was because the other team was trying to poison us in an effort to beat us. Anyways, we played our game, had our customary end of game hand shake, and then Blake approached everyone on our team and handed out free cards for each of our team members and their family members entitling everyone to a free dinner from the *Curry Up Now* truck. What? No scam? No secret agenda? As it turns out, Intapp was having a company meeting and just thought it would be cool to do something nice. That's it. No secret agenda. Nada. Our team was amazed as we watched Blake hand out the free dinner cards and we all slowly walked (ok, some people on our team ran their asses off) towards the humungous orange and red truck.

My son Seattle and daughter Gracia had never eaten from a roach coach, I mean mobile truck before and they were both jumping up and down at the idea as if the Easter Bunny had just given them a 100 pound bag of jelly beans. We approached the truck and I started to focus on the truck and its design. I've never seen an orange and red roach coach before. This truck had cool graphics and a funny catchy name - *Curry Up Now.* I thought to myself, what the heck, this mobile food truck is promoting itself on Twitter, Facebook, YouTube, Flickr, and Yelp. The guy behind the counter proudly and happily introduced himself as Amir one of the founders of *Curry Up Now*. Amir was upbeat, high energy and I could tell had a commitment to customer service and making people feel good. It was at this time I knew that Amir and *Curry Up Now* gets it! They not only know how to make great Indian Street Food (I'm not sure what street food is) but they really understand marketing and how to make a great customer experience.

Take Away: What are you doing to market your business and tilt the playing field to your advantage? In marketing terms, what is your Unique Selling Proposition? What are you doing to make your business stand out and look different than the competition?   What are you doing to bridge old school marketing with new school social media? Let's get back to *Curry Up Now*. If you own a roach coach, do you paint it white like everyone else, or do you paint it orange and red? Do you use the side of the truck as a cool mural to draw attention to your truck or do you have large blank spaces covered with road grime? Do you have the icons for the different Facebook, Twitter, YouTube, Flickr and Yelp social media sites displayed where your customers can easily see them? Do you have a sales staff that truly wants to help customers have a great experience? And finally do you have good food? Like I said, I don't even know what Indian Street Food is, but I do know if I see the *Curry Up Now* mobile food truck at Greer Park again I will have no hesitation eating some more of Amir's food and will have zero hesitation in recommending it to anyone else. Got a run and post a 5 star Yelp recommendation for *Curry Up Now*.

Only IDIOTS Get Run Over by Steam Rollers. DON'T Be the Social Media Ostrich That Gets Run Over by the Steam Roller of Change

Over and over again I hear small business owners say *"I don't have time to use social media to market and grow my business."* When I question these same business owners about the tons of money they must be making from all their other successful efforts, they all almost always reply that their income is far below what they desire. I then share two thoughts with them: either you're wasting your time with some activities that don't add to the bottom line, or you're using the wrong tools to grow your business.

True Story. In the spring of 2011, I was invited by Matt Johnson of Intero Real Estate - Evergreen in San Jose, CA to train a group of real estate agents in setting up their social media campaigns. The group of ten agents met for five 2-hour sessions where they learned how to make an Animoto video, how to set up their Google and Yelp business profiles, set up their Facebook Business pages, how to set up a WordPress blog and how to set up their

LinkedIn business profile. We also shared how to write content that the major search engines like to crawl and index. I also shared with them many of the small business marketing tips I had learned in the past 25 years.

I also shared the following fictitious story with them:

Business owner A (Open Minded to adapting to change) tells Business Owner B (Too Busy to change my present behavior) that she is going to change her marketing plan and move forward with the goal of using a social media campaign to dominate the market space that she and **Too Busy** will share. **Open Minded** decides to hop on the Social Media Steam Roller of change which travels one mile/hour, 24 hours/day, 7 days/week, and 365 days/year. She starts her fictitious social media journey in San Diego and heads north to San Jose (approximately 400 miles away) where **Too Busy** is running his butt off with little business success.

At the end of Day 1, Open Minded calls Too Busy and lets him know she is now near Camp Pendleton and has learned how to make and post a video to YouTube. All she got was Too Busy's response, *"So what."*

At the end of Day 2, Open Minded calls Too Busy again and lets him know she's now in Orange County and that she has just set up a WordPress Blog and made her first blog post. Too Busy's response is as brief as previously, he simply said *"Big Deal."*

At the end of Day 3, Open Minded calls Too Busy again and lets him know she's now in Long Beach and that she has just set up a Facebook Personal and Business Page and made her first wall posts. This time Too Busy sarcastically responds with *"So tell me about the new business you've gained with all your wasted efforts."*

At the end of Day 4, Open Minded calls Too Busy again and lets him know she's now at LAX and that she has just received a message on Facebook that one of her friends is referring a client to her and that the friend had forgotten that Open Minded worked in that business. This time Too Busy once again sarcastically responds with *"Yeah, yeah, yeah. Let me know once you really get some new business."*

Over the next two weeks, the journey continues with Open Minded consistently adding new tools to her social media campaign as she gets closer and closer to San Jose.

As the next two weeks wind down, Open Minded has now traveled to Morgan Hill just 15 miles south of San Jose. She lets Too Busy know that she will be arriving in San Jose the next day with her new social media campaign in place and on maintenance mode. Now, Open Minded has created the following tools in her social media campaign: a blog, she has a personal and business Facebook profile, a YouTube Channel, a Yelp account, Google, Yahoo and Microsoft business profiles, many local merchant profiles, has built a search engine optimized LinkedIn profile, has linked her blog to her old school website, has posted eight blog posts; she has commented on 52 other blogs besides her own.   And guess what? The referral from her friend on Facebook just signed a contract for Open Minded to represent her in a business transaction.

As Open Minded arrives in San Jose, Too Busy replies, *"Wow. I can't believe the results you're getting. Can you show me how to start?"* And Open Minded replies, *"Sorry, I don't have the time right now. I'm busy servicing my Facebook referral."*

Note: True Story. Three weeks after the real Social Media class finished at Intero Real Estate, Monique Bosomworth, an agent in the office was contacted by four potential buyers who found her through her newly posted social media efforts.

Take Away: Don't be the ostrich business owner that gets run over by the Social Media Steam Roller and then gets his ass kicked by the competition. Get yourself and your business online. In this world of stiff competition, it is next to impossible to to win if you are not visible on the different social media sites.

Does Your Computer have a Social Media Transmitted Disease? The Danger of Third Party Apps and Free iPads

Ever received an e-mail from a Nigerian Prince asking for your help with a complex 10 million dollar inheritance transaction? Have you ever clicked on a link to Southwest Airlines on your computer and been taken to a page asking if you would like to use your Facebook account to login to their site? Or how about receiving a post on your Facebook wall announcing how your best bud from high school just received a free iPad and so can you? If you haven't received such wonderful communications from the noble Nigerian, my favorite airline, or your high school class clown, then it's just a matter of time until you join the club.

What's going on with all this stuff? In the case of the "Noble Nigerian", he's just trying to sucker you into a scam where he gets your financial info so that he can suck you bone dry financially in one of the stupidest scams in the world. If you fall for this, it's either you probably don't deserve to hold on to your finances or you have one foot in the door to the local Alzheimer's clinic. In the case of the Southwest Airlines and free iPad scenario, someone has hijacked your friends FB account and is out to scam you.

Recently, the editor of the Palo Alto Free Press asked me to write a guest blog about the *Dangers of Third Party Apps* built for sites like Twitter or Facebook. Third Party Apps are those special programs that allow you to expand the functionality of your social media sites and complement a program (first party app) written by another business such as Facebook or Twitter. My favorite third party app I like to use is HootSuite for scheduling my social media posts.

Other kinds of third party apps you may have heard of are called plug-ins or add-ons. Perhaps you have a WordPress blog and you want to insert a photo contest in to your blog -- there's a third party app for that. Or, perhaps you want to add an e-commerce page on your website -- there's a third party app for that too.

So what's the danger of Third Party Apps and clicking on that link to get a free Southwest Airline ticket or free iPad? In the case of many third party apps, you are requested to give access to your Facebook, Twitter or other social media account -- confidential and private information including login information. In some cases, you give access to your complete e-mail directory and allow the app provider access to all your contact e-mail addresses while waiving your right to protect this information. I personally do not know of an instance where the people in my e-mail directory have received an unauthorized e-mail through me, and as far as I know I've never posted a message saying I've just won a free iPad on my friend's walls on Facebook.

So here are the two big deals I see: first issue, I've heard of third party app developers selling their businesses to another business. Who's to say the new owner of the app on your computer has the same high standards as the first business that developed the app in the first place? Some people believe this is where their info can be compromised and used against them. Is my confidential info now owned by someone I don't even know?

Second issue, this involves those free Southwest Airline tickets, the free iPads, and that question, "Would you like to know who's looking at your profile on Facebook?" (FYI, Facebook specifically prohibits third party app companies from accessing who is looking at whose profile).

Most of these too good to be true offers and questions are really just companies trying to get you to answer questionnaires - ...where the company asking the question gets paid for each questionnaire successfully completed. Their goal is to get you to open the post, answer it, and have the post delivered to your friends. In turn have them repeat the cycle. For most people silly enough to click on these free offers, the only result is having to send an embarrassing message to all your friends letting them know you screwed up.

Not sure about which of those Facebook offers are legitimate? Check out FaceCrooks.com or Like FaceCrooks on Facebook. *FaceCrooks* is a site that tracks which of those posts are legit or a bunch of B.S.

Take Away: Be careful which third party apps you install on your computer or tie in to your social media sites. Make sure you like FaceCrooks. Tim and his crew at FaceCrooks can save you a lot of time, perhaps some money and some embarrassment. Anyway, I gotta run, I just got an e-mail from Nigeria requesting that I fly to another city using my free

Southwest Airlines ticket and that there will be a free iPad waiting for me at the airport check-in stand. Life is too good to be true!

Blogging

What Da Heck is HTML? Hyper Text Mark-Up Language or Hard To Manage Language

If you have a business website when was the last time you made a change to the content on your website? Was it in the last week? The last two weeks? The last month? Three months ago? If you're like most of the business owners I meet, it's been over three months since you've changed anything on your website. Why don't most business owners make changes to their website? It's because most business owners don't know HTML and don't change the content on their websites because they don't know how.

In my opinion, HTML stands for HARD TO MANAGE LANGUAGE. In reality HTML is a language that prevents biz owners from managing their web presence themselves and keeps lots of HTML programmers employed.

I don't care if you're a brain surgeon, plumber, a hairdresser, mechanic or birthday party clown; if you want people to become your customers, it's becoming increasingly important to have a web presence where you regularly change content on your website to rank at the top of the search engines. If you don't rank high on the first page of Google your business will have a low probability of being contacted by prospective customers. Your site will languish on the search engine rankings and be cast off to the "sandbox" – the place where websites and businesses, which are not on the first page of Google, die a sad death.

So if you're wondering what you should do to get more traffic to your website and a higher ranking on the search engines, you should consider using a blog. Blogs are websites. Let me say it again and you should remember this - Blogs are websites. One last time for my ADD friends – blogs are websites. It is now easy to build a website that looks like an old school HTML website that is built so that busy business owners can change content, add pictures and videos without having to call or hire a webmaster.

The most common blogging platform in the world is WordPress. Other popular blogging platforms include Blogger and Tumblr. I have taught hundreds of business owners how to create WordPress blogs (remember a blog is a website) in under two hours. WordPress is easy to use, easy to make changes to, easy to add videos and pictures to and has all kinds of cool features that allow you to add e-commerce features, coupons, surveys, contests and other cool features. There is now a worldwide army of WordPress designers who can help you customize your blog.

Take Away: The cool thing about using a blogging platform for your website is that if done correctly, you will get more traffic to your site because you will actually make changes to the website, you will rank higher on the search engines (which means you will most likely kick your competitors in the ass) and you will be free of having to pay a webmaster to make changes to your website.

Take Away: Remember if you want to play in a sandbox - go to the park -not the second page of Google.

Widgets and White Wall Tires - Don't Re-Invent the Wheel When Using WordPress

What's a widget? When your car, bicycle, skateboard or roller blades need new wheels do you make them yourself? Or do you buy them and then install them? Since the first caveman invented the wheel, most people have chosen not to re-invent the wheel and instead copy the idea and use it to make their life more efficient and easy. Widgets are to your website as wheels are to cars. Just as tires are easily installed on your car, widgets are small chunks of existing code designed for a specific purpose that are easily installed on your website.

The cool thing about installing widgets on your website is that you don't need to know any programming languages and that it can be added, removed or rearranged by clicking and dragging your mouse around. You don't need to know HTML and you don't need to hire someone at $100/hour to install them. In my opinion, it's actually easier for most people to install a widget on their website than it is to change a tire on their car.

Need to add a form to your website? Want to host a website visitor photo contest? Want to have Tweets of happy customers posted to your website? Need to add Google Maps to your website? A calendar? How about a Facebook Like button? Most likely for whatever widget you can dream up someone has already invented it and it lies just a few clicks away from having in integrated in your website.

Have you ever been on a website and you see the icons for all the different social media sites are scrolling up and down the page with you? This feature was created using a Floating Social Media Widget. This widget allows you to have the different social media icons constantly located in your site visitors view and makes it super easy for them to share your information. Since the whole idea of social media is to share valuable information why not make it easy for your content to be shared on Facebook, Twitter, Pinterest, YouTube, LinkedIn, on an RSS Feed or Google+?

Take Away: Be smarter than the caveman who invented the wheel! Don't re-invent the wheel and before you learn how to change a tire on your car, learn how to use widgets.

Left, Right, Left How to make Your Blog Sticky and Look Sexy

We've all read papers or documents with no photos and that look like the terms and conditions of a mortgage application. They look boring, they don't appeal to the eye, and if possible people just scan them and move on as fast as possible. For most people to stay on a site (stickiness) the site must be appealing to eyes: which means the posts should be short and contain eye candy. With your blog you literally have microseconds to either hook a reader or drive them away. So what the heck does *Left, Right, Left* have to do with my posts and making my site sticky?

If you want people to read your blog or stay on your website there are three rules I suggest you follow:

Rule One: Use the *Left, Right, Left Rule* - start the blog with an image just to the left of the first word in the first paragraph. With the second paragraph post a picture to the right of the paragraph. And finally I like to the end the post with an image to the left of the last paragraph. Whenever possible I try to limit my blog posts to three paragraphs.

Rule Two: Most experts believe a blog should be approximately 250 - 450 words in length. People have limited attention spans and won't spend a lot of time reading endless rambling posts. They want info quickly and they want to be entertained. Blog writing should be to the point and in most cases written in a casual tone.

Rule Three: **Format the important words** in your post **using the bold feature.** This **makes the post pop to the eye** and makes it look interesting. Bolding key words add sizzle to your text and helps make your site sticky. Using blue colored hyperlinks also draws eyes to your post and hooks your reader to read even more of your content.

If you want to dominate on the search engines using your blog you should post on a regular basis (cadence). There should be some correlation between the name of the blog post and the content of the post. Keyword density should be 2-4% of total words in the post. FYI, keyword density is the number of times the keywords appear in the post. For example, if the post is 200 words, the keywords in your post are about juggling - the word "juggling" should appear 4-8 times in the post. If you haven't read the chapter *Don't be an Old Dog – Learn to Blog*, you should check it out after finishing this chapter.

Take Away: People get bored quickly and they like eye candy. If you want people to stay on your blog (sticky), get marching (Left, Right, Left) and make your blog visually appealing. Strategically placed photos and the highlighting key words will get more eyeballs spending more time on your site.

Don't Be an Old Dog - Learn How to Blog

Whoever said *"You can't teach an old dog new tricks"* probably doesn't own a dog, doesn't own a cell phone or doesn't own a Facebook account. Anyone who owns a dog, who shuts off the TV and grabs a handful of their dog's favorite treats, knows that you can teach almost any dog to do anything in 30 minutes. So here's a very important question you may not have been asked in the past 10 years — are you willing to learn a few new tricks to grow your business or do you have one foot in the doggie graveyard?

Don't underestimate the importance of having a strong web presence for you and your business. If you want to grow your business, people must be able to find you and your business on Google. People use Google in two ways when making their decisions on whom or which they will do business with.

First, people may search for your type of business when they don't have a recommendation from a friend. For example, a web surfer who doesn't know a realtor and is looking to buy a home in Palo Alto may enter "homes for sale in Palo Alto, CA" into the Google search box.

Wouldn't you want this potential client to find you as the best realtor in Palo Alto?

Second, people who have heard of you or your business may "Google" your name in an effort to see what people are saying about you or your business. In the realtor example just used, the same web surfer may then go back to Google and type in your name, profession and geographic location in an effort to do more research and to help them decide if they want to contact you or not.

For most small businesses, blogging is the easiest way to climb up the search engine rankings and to dominate the business' online niche. To me, a properly created blog is nothing more than a website that allows a business owner to publish useful information that Google loves and allows your business to rank on the top of the search engine results for your niche. The cool thing about blogs is that you don't need to know any special programming language *(see What Da Heck is HTML? Hyper Text Mark-up Language or Hard to Manage Language)* and you don't need a web designer to create one. The most commonly used blogging platforms are WordPress, Tumblr and Blogger.

According to HubSpot (if you're interested in growing your business using online marketing you should go LIKE HubSpot on Facebook after reading this chapter – HubSpot has tons a free ebooks on growing your business) companies that blog get 55% more website visitors than companies that don't blog and get 97% more inbound links compared to companies that don't blog.

<u>Take Away:</u> For most businesses blogging is the fastest, easiest, most cost effective way to rise in the search engines. And for those business owners that also own dogs remember that while you're out walking your dog, your competitor may be out there learning new blogging tricks that will kick your business in the butt.

Getting Found on Google

Thoreau and Shakespeare - Where art thou Keywords: 5 Writing Tips in Getting Found on the Search Engines

Writing for search engines requires the use of strategically placed keywords if your goal is getting found on Google. I think if Thoreau and Shakespeare were hired by one of Silicon Valley's, oops I mean, Social Media Valley's bleeding edge companies, they would be out of job in no time. Sorry Thoreau, no Walden Pond here; and sorry Shakespeare, nobody gives a hoot about iambic pentameter. As a matter of fact, the door is over there and don't let it hit you in the Keister on the way out!

Ready for some lessons in SEO? Here's are a few tips.

1. Use Keywords in Your Different Site Urls and Names

    Getting found on Google requires the strategic use of keywords when setting up your business profiles on Facebook, Twitter, YouTube and your blog. Also, set up your professional profile on LinkedIn and use this LinkedIn trick for inserting keywords in your profile. Whenever possible, use keywords in your Url and in the name of your site. For example, with Web Lunch Box the website url is www.WebLunchBox.com, and the name of the site is Web Lunch Box — naming the URL and the site name both Web Lunch Box lets Google know these are important keywords for our business getting found on Google. This same process was used with naming our Twitter account and YouTube account with Web Lunch Box in the name. It's important to make sure all your company profiles are public so that the search engines can crawl over your site.

2. Use Keywords in your Post Titles and in the content of all your writing. In addition to using keywords in your different site urls and social media profiles, you should use keywords in the name of your blog posts and in the content on your different sites, profiles and blog posts. For example, for the name of this post I've used the following keywords: "Keywords" and "Getting Found on Google" in the post title and have used the keywords throughout this post. Note: A keyword can be more than one word; and keywords are often separated by commas when tagging content.

3. Use Keywords In The First Sentence of Your Blog Posts. Look at the first sentence of this post: "Writing for search engines requires the use of strategically placed keywords if your goal is getting found on Google." The keyword/s getting found on Google were intentionally placed there so that when Google crawls over the post, it will identify that the keywords are used in the name of the post and in the first sentence. FYI, manner bloggers bold keywords in their posts.

4. Be Relevant and Timely. Recently, I had the privilege of co-sponsoring Gary Vaynerchuk at a speaking

engagement and book signing event at Kepler's Books and Magazines in Menlo Park, CA. In addition to Gary Vaynerchuk promoting the event on his own Facebook page and web sites; Web Lunch Box promoted the event on its Facebook page, on the Home Town Peninsula Website and even promoted the event to 757 business students at the Stanford School of Business. By being relevant to the publicized The Thank You Economy event at Kepler's, the Web Lunch Box posts were seen as being more relevant to this popular event.

5. Write in a Style That You Attract Followers and Sharers of Your Content. The more followers you have on your different social media sites, the better. The real goal is to get lots of followers who also become great sharers of your information. Once you master the art of writing interesting, educating information in a fun-to-read format, you'll find people will start to share your content. Once you get lots of followers and sharers of your content, Google will look at your site (or sites) as being relevant and authoritative. To make sharing your information easy, make sure you include lots of links and share buttons on your site.

Want to Become a Member of The Upwardly Mobile Business Owners Club? Optimizing Your Business Website for Mobile Browsing

I was one of those weird students who liked Statistics 101 when they took it in college. While taking statistics in the evening at Framingham State College, I was able to actually use my new found statistics psycho garb at my nowhere-leading job at Coatings Engineering in Sudbury, Massachusetts. Today, I have no interest in standard deviations and confidence levels of different statistical samples; however I do use statistics to guide me in my business decisions. Unless you're a bored nerd with an affinity for numbers like me, DON'T go out and sign up for statistics like I did. Use statistics that already exist and are just a click away. To save you some time I've gathered some stats you can't ignore:

- Half of U.S. Adults have smartphones (can access the internet)
- 90% of these adults use their smartphones to send e-mails and surf the web
- 22 - 25%% of U.S. web searches are on mobile devices
- Only 26% of U.S. businesses have a mobile optimized website

- 1/3 of at home internet searches are done on the smartphone, not the home computer because the person doesn't have high speed internet access at home
- Only 60% of U.S. businesses have a website
- 3% of the U.S. population are millionaires

All of my statistics above came from the internet and took me about five minutes to assemble. I don't know which statistics are exactly true or accurate, and frankly I don't care. Every single stat I found had other similar numbers and different sources. I do know these numbers, even if statistically off by a small margin, are too big to ignore and they show a trend. I also believe these numbers are only going to increase. If you ignore these numbers and don't figure out how to use them to your advantage, it will be just a matter of time before one of your competitors does and whacks your business upside the head. That's it. Statistics show the world's population is using mobile devices more and more to find information, share information and make purchases.

Okay, now that you just took my Statistics class, let's move on to English class with Professor Tim. In my English class we don't care about *Catcher In the Rye* or *Moby Dick*. We don't care about Walden Pond and we don't care about *50 Shades of Grey*. We care about words and writing techniques that make our businesses money. We care about words that make our dreams come true and words that make the world a better place. In my English class we care about keywords, names of Urls, names of blogs and blog post titles, hyperlinks, keyword density and how to use Google Analytics, and Alexa.com.

We also care about words that didn't exist 10 years ago. Words like *Mobify*. Can you say Mo-b-fi? Mobify. Mobify means making sure your website is formatted for mobile devices. Your mobile website must be easy to read and use if you want to convert all those coffee shop web surfers to paying customers. Mofiby. Class dismissed.

Okay, you're probably saying *"Great, but how do I get started with building my business mobile site?"* I've found that www.hottogomo.com, a Google web site, is in my opinion the best and quickest introductory site to getting you up to speed on what to do. Before you pay a single penny to any website designer, make sure you visit this site - it can save you time, save you money, help tilt the playing field to your business' advantage and help convert prospects into paying customers.

I'm a firm believer in WordPress as a platform for building a business' website. Some advantages are that a WordPress site can be set up in a couple of hours, you don't need to know HTML and there already exists tools for mobifying your website (if you haven't read my chapter *What Da Heck is HTML? Hyper Text Mark-Up Language or Hard to Manage Language?*, make sure you read it after reading this chapter).

For my brothers and sisters in business who use WordPress, I suggest you go to www.wpbeginner.com and read *11 Ways to Create a Mobile Friendly WordPress Site*. A cool thing about these WordPress tools are that they detect when someone is thumping on your website from a mobile device and makes sure the web surfer is given the mobified version of your website.

Take Away: The world is going mobile. If you want to join the ranks of wealthy upwardly mobile business owners (remember my stat above about 3% of Americans being millionaires) make sure you mobify your website. Don't go out and study statistics and don't read Moby Dick. Read about Mobifying your business site.

Tim's Top Ten Small Business Resources & People to Important to Ignore

~~David Lettermen's~~ Tim's Top Ten Small Business Resources & People too Important to Ignore

Unlike the printed version of The Yellow Pages Directory (which in my opinion is nothing more than a door stop), this directory of resources is full of useful stuff to help you succeed in life and business. They're not in any special order; I just started typing away and this is the order in which I thought of them. BTW, yes I know there are more than 10 items on my list - I just liked the alliteration with the three T's in the title of this chapter - Tim's Top Ten.

Duct Tape Marketing   www.ducttapemarketing.com

Duct Tape Marketing is a website full of info on managing your small business and is the brain child of John Jantsch. In addition to offering paid speaking/consulting work, John Jantsch's site is full of practical and free e-books, is straight to the point, and is written in a roll up your sleeves and jump in style. John is smart, witty and sometimes funny (think of it, who in his right mind would name his business Duct Tape Marketing?)

Recommendation: Follow Duct Tape Marketing on Facebook and check out the Duct Tape Marketing website.

Karen Salmansohn   www.notsalmon.com

Life is too short not to live balls to the walls and learn from others who truly have a zest for life and reach out to help others. I find Karen Salmanshon's artwork and posts to always be inspirational and on point. I don't know Karen personally, but if I did, I'd give her a big hug and ask her to go skate boarding in Central Park. I think Karen's own words best state what her life and website are about. "My mission in one long run on sentence: To offer easy-to-absorb insights and advice to help you bloom into your happiest, most loved, highest potential self – and have fun in the process – because I use playful analogies, feisty humor, and stylish graphics to distill big ideas (from the latest scientific studies to ancient wisdom) into short, easily-digestible, life-changing tips".

Recommendation: Go find Karen Salmansohn on FB or on her website and add her fun wisdom to your tabletop of life's salt and pepper shakers and see how your life tastes afterwards. Yummy!

Social Media Examiner   www.socialmediaexaminer.com

In my opinion, Social Media Examiner is the number one online source for learning how to use social media to grow your business. Social Media Examiner was started by Michael Stelzner, a fellow social media evangelist, has over 120,000 followers on Facebook; his is ranked one of the top five most read business blogs. Don't let the site's simple graphics and jungle safari theme fool you. There's plenty of excellent, timely content there. Kudos to Michael Stelzner!

Recommendation: Follow Social Media Examiner on Facebook and if you're a hardcore social media nerd, check out Social Media Examiner's conferences.

Bob Parsons, Founder of GoDaddy.com   www.BobParsons.me

Bob Parsons is my favorite no-nonsense, no screwing around, business founder I follow on social media. All my websites are hosted by GoDaddy.com and I find the GoDaddy customer service second to none. If I had to pick a Dean of the Business School for Busy Business Owners, it would definitely be Bob Parsons. You might not like the GoDaddy.com racy ads during the Super Bowl, but if you haven't read any of Bob's blog posts or haven't read a copy of his _16 Rules for Success in Business and Life in General_, you should hop on it now.

Recommendation: Go to www.BobParsons.me and read everything you can.

HubSpot   www.HubSpot.com

I love HubSpot. Besides being located in my old stomping ground Boston, MA (okay, Cambridge), HubSpot totally knows how to use social media and is the best example as far as I know of giving something away free to get paying customers. HubSpot is in the business of helping other businesses grow through SEO, inbound marketing campaigns, e-mail marketing and website analytics. HubSpot.tv is always full of fun, useful information. And for all you old MC Hammer fans, they even conducted an interview with Mr. "You Can't Touch This" on how he uses social media to grow his business. They offer many free, useful e-books and infographics on how the business world is changing.

Recommendation: Check out HubSpot on FB, watch some HubSpot.tv instead of Jerry Springer, check out HubSpot's business tools and if you're in the Boston area have a beer for me at the Cask n' Flagon.

Gary Vaynerchuk   www.GaryVaynerchuk.com

I don't drink wine, but I guzzle down Gary's business advice in cases. Gary is an extremely successful business owner, writer, blogger and if you ask him, the future owner of the New York Jets football team. I've met Gary and had the opportunity to interview him. I found him to be "Johnny on the Spot" when it comes to business strategy. If you're faint at heart or have ears that have never heard a swear word, then you should run like hell from Gary Vee. He has a mouth like a drunken sailor but has a heart full of passion and a sincerity that's bigger than Donald Trump's ego.

Recommendation: If you drink, get a glass of wine and go to GaryVaynerchuk.com and do some surfing or go read a copy of The Thank You Economy or Crush It! If you don't drink, go to GaryVaynerchuk.com and do some surfing or go read a copy of The Thank You Economy or Crush It! It's that important, so you don't have a choice.

Dr. Oz   Realage.com

If you're not living a healthy lifestyle; if you are worried about your health, or if you want to maximize your fitness level, you must go to RealAge now. Dr. Mehmet Oz, from the TV show, "The Dr. Oz Show", along with some of his buddies, developed RealAge.com. It's a website where you take a test regarding your lifestyle decisions and how they affect your life expectancy. After you complete the short test, the site calculates your real age in medical years (not how many years you've been alive) and to what age you can expect to live, based on current lifestyle decisions. For example, you could be a 28-year-old who in medical years is really 47; or you could be like me, a 54-year-old whose real age in medical years is 47.

Recommendation: If you don't want to meet the Grim Reaper any earlier than you have to, go to Realage.com, take the test, and get your life moving in a new direction. Who knows? Maybe Dr. Oz can help add more years to your life and you can delay your appointment with the Grim Reaper. Also, check out my chapter: Fat Man Skinny Man Meet Thunder Thighs – Exercise and Business Success.

Marie Forleo   www.marieforleo.com

Marie Forleo rocks and lives outside the normal biz model box! From Marie TV to her Biz School she's one biz lady who wears her heart and soul on her ~~shirt~~, I mean blouse sleeve. She's a networking maven, who delivers rich meaningful content all with a big smile. Oh yeah, she's not too proud to laugh at herself (watch the end of each edition of Marie TV and you'll know what I mean). Her site seems to be geared to women, but what the heck, I find value in her material.

Recommendation: Go to MarieForleo.com and sign up for Marie Forleo's weekly blast of content and entertainment. You won't be unhappy with your decision and you'll be glad you've decided to follow this Jersey girl instead of Snooki and JaWow!

Timothy Ferriss   www.TimothyFerriss.com

Timothy Ferriss is best known for his book *The Four Hour Work Week: Escape 9-5, Live Anywhere,* and *Join the New Rich.* Even though this book is 5-6 years old, I still listen to this book 2-3 times per year while running the Dish at Stanford University. This book is really about the most valuable possession you own -- your time. Yes, you can read the book and try to create a four-hour work week for yourself, or you can do what I did -- focus on reducing the time to do tasks, reduce the cost of doing things. This frees up money for other things. Use the stories for inspiration and good entertainment.   Tim Ferriss definitely thinks outside the box and lives a life most small business owners would love to have.

Recommendation: Buy or download a copy of The Four Hour Work Week, go for a run, and learn how to start saving some time and learn how to use your time differently and efficiently. BTW, be careful if Tim Ferriss challenges you to a dance or kick boxing contest. He will take the time to figure out how to kick you in the butt.

Monday Morning Mojo
www.interomojo.com/category/monday-morning-mojo/

Tom Tognoli is one of the most inspirational people I've been blessed to meet and call a friend. He's sincere and bright, one of the best communicators I know and knows how to manage time better than anyone I know. He wears his heart and soul on his sleeve and I'd follow him any day into battle. Tom knows how to make others see the best in themselves. Every Monday morning, I receive an e-mail from Tom with his latest version of Monday Morning Mojo. I not only receive his e-mail, but look forward to getting it. Hey, it's the first e-mail I open every Monday! For me, receiving Monday Morning Mojo is like having Vince Lombardi, Tony Robbins or Jim Harbaugh send me a personal e-mail with some reflection that is relevant to my life. Monday Morning Mojo is not just a soft read like a lot of the stuff you see on Facebook, it's a great read with an action item. I strongly suggest you subscribe to Tom Tognoli's Monday Morning Mojo and if you follow what Tom has to say, your life will never be the same. BTW, I've found other Monday Morning Mojos on the web – but the one I rave about is written by Tom Tognoli.

Recommendation: Sign up for Monday Morning Mojo and if you're ever in the San Francisco Bay Area and are in the real estate business, call Tom up at his Intero Real Estate office in Saratoga, CA and go meet him. I promise you your life will not be the same.

ThinkTQ.com   www.thinktq.com

I'm a firm believer that time is your most valuable resource. ThinkTQ.com is a free website offering a test that measures how you use your time. In a nutshell, it measures your time quotient. It's like Realage.com, but instead of measuring your health, ThinkTQ.com measures how you spend your time; it then offers suggestions on how you can improve your ability to manage time. The first time I took the ThinkTQ.com time management test, I felt the folks from ThinkTQ.com had been following me around for a year, recording everything I did when it came to how I managed my time. This site is a must if you're dedicated to being the best you can be.

Recommendation: Find the time in the next 24 hours to take the ThinkTQ.com time management test. You'll be amazed and most likely   shocked on how you've been wasting time.

Tim Davis   www.facebook.com/timwdavis

Michael Jordan and Joe Montana had a coach - if you're looking for a business coach check out Tim Davis. Tim is constantly throwing positive stuff at the universe through his FB page. Tim is direct yet compassionate. Tim's faith in God is deeper than the Grand Canyon and his commitment to others is unending. If you're looking for sound business advice, check out Tim Davis at his Facebook page.

Recommendation: Follow Tim on FB and start using the advice he gives shares. If you're in the mortgage business don't be a Barny and not follow Tim. One other thing – whatever you do don't let Tim go clothes shopping for you – he wears the strangest socks and jackets of anyone I know.

Yep I built This   www.facebook.com/YepIBuiltThis

I just love this Facebook page. Yep I Built This is a site where entrepreneurs and small business owners can profile their business on FB. Each day, Yep I Built This features an inspirational start-up story. If you need to share some positive mojo with your fellow Brothers and Sistas in small business, you can't go wrong here. With more than 225,000 Facebook likes, Yep I Built This just makes you feel good about being in business yourself.

Recommendation: Go follow Yep I Built This on FB; but more importantly, go build a business that you'd be proud to showcase on Yep I Built This.

Jurgen Weller   www.facebook.com/jurgen.weller

Jurgen Weller (I call him Dr. J) is a master of how to use FB to engage people. Jurgen has an uncanny ability to post stuff that makes you want to read more of his content, be the best you can be, and kick ass in business. Dr. J also has a special post he does every Friday called "Romantic Fridays." I know it sounds corny, but I always find a nugget of wisdom in his "Romantic Fridays" post that I think Dr. Ruth would be proud of. A big shout out to Dr. J and good luck if you're trying to friend Jurgen Weller on FB.

Recommendation: Follow Jurgen on FB, read "Romantic Fridays" and watch your biz and love life take off.

About Tim Hmelar

The Mumbo Jumbo and Blah, Blah, Blah

Tim Hmelar: The Mumbo Jumbo and Blah, Blah, Blah

Tim Hmelar (last name pronounced Mil-lar) is a serial entrepreneur and small business owner who lives in Palo Alto, CA. Tim is the owner of The Kitchen & Bath Company of Palo Alto and has been providing construction services to homeowners in the Greater Palo Alto area since 1980.

Tim's first real venture in small business was taking a semester off from school and helping his brother Frank orchestrate a leveraged buyout of a plastics company in Sudbury, Massachusetts. Tim literally used his textbooks in finance, operations research, business law and statistics to help his brother in the purchasing and setting up of the new company.

Tim has also had some business successes and some business failures of his own. His successes include running a construction company where Tim has had the opportunity to work on the homes of some of the San Francisco Bay Area's most well-known business leaders including the CEOs of Google, Hewlett Packard and Cisco. Tim also co-founded Web Lunch Box a social media training company. After having a tumor removed from his back and assessing how best to use his time; Tim decided to only juggle one business ball and focus all his efforts on his construction business and his family. Web Lunch Box is no longer a business but the FB page still exists where Tim still gives biz and social media advice and commentary from time to time. Tim also unsuccessfully started a real estate company in Mexico and an online coupon company (Ouch!!!).

Tim is a graduate of San Jose State University. He has taken courses at the following schools: Northeastern University, Framingham State College, Foothill Junior College, De Anza College, Mission College, West Valley College, Stanford University (Continuing Ed.), UC Berkeley (Continuing Ed) and most importantly the School of Hard Knocks. Tim is a lifelong learner who believes one's education must never end if he wishes to stay relevant.

Tim enjoys spending both his personal and professional time with compassionate, giving people who share their talents in an effort to make the world a better place. Tim does NOT enjoy spending time with self-centered people who do not share their talents with others. Tim's favorite business attire is a white dress shirt with blue jeans and cowboy boots. He also likes to wear baseball caps and Van's sneakers.

Tim is passionate about life and business. He likes to teach and talk. Sometimes Tim talks too much. Tim has been a guest speaker at many meetings, conferences and universities including San Jose State University and Stanford University. Tim is a blogger and television host who has hosted shows for KMVT in Mountain View, CA. Tim also has been a radio guest and is often a quoted resource for many newspapers and magazines.

Tim's spiritual/religious belief is that all people have strengths and weaknesses, and that the purpose of life is to be a loving person with everyone you meet. Tim believes people have the right to believe in any God they desire provided they not twist religious teachings to hurt others. While at San Jose State

University, Tim traveled to Europe, Asia and Africa; he read everything he could get his hands on about many of the world's different religions, and also books about Ghandi, Martin Luther King and Malcom X.

When not spending time with his family, Tim enjoys running The Dish at Stanford University, playing softball, lifting weights, watching the 49ers, SF Giants, Oakland A's and the San Jose Sharks (BTW, Tim still wants to know why the Sharks can't win the Stanley Cup). Tim also enjoys hanging out at the beach in San Diego and Mexico.

Tim enjoys coaching youth sports, where kids are taught the fundamentals of sports and good sportsmanship. Tim believes that kids who work hard, focus on the fundamentals, and commit to the team are most likely to experience winning and success later in life. Tim doesn't like youth coaches or parents who focus only on winning or getting straight A's.

Tim's hair is graying and thinning; he has some wrinkles and needs to wear glasses to read. He has to watch what he eats in order to maintain his waist line. Tim's greatest vices are cheese and chocolate. Tim is happy to be alive; he is grateful to have his family, great friends, a roof over his head, his faith, and his health.

And now if you've read all this, I suggest you go out and start improving your business and life.

www.BusinessSchoolForBusyBusinessOwners.com